WHERE THE TRUTH IS FOUND

Edward Knapp-Fisher was born in London in 1915, and educated at King's School, Worcester, Trinity College, Oxford, and Wells Theological College. He was made deacon in 1939 and ordained priest in 1940. After a curacy at Brighouse in Yorkshire, he served as a RNVR Chaplain until the end of the war. He became Chaplain of Cuddesdon Theological College in 1946, and Chaplain of St John's College, Cambridge, in 1948. In 1952 he returned to Cuddesdon as Principal, and he was consecrated Bishop of Pretoria in 1960.

In 1975 he was appointed to a Canonry at Westminster Abbey. His particular interest is in systematic theology and ecumenism. He has published three other books, and has been an Anglican member of the Anglican/Roman Catholic International Commission since its formation in 1969. He was married in 1965.

WHERE THE TRUTH IS FOUND

Some Reflections on the Way of the World

E. G. KNAPP-FISHER

Change and decay in all around I see;
O Thou, who changest not, abide with me!
H. F. Lyte

Collins
FONTANA BOOKS

First published in Fontana 1975

© E. G. Knapp-Fisher 1975

Made and printed in Great Britain
William Collins Sons & Co Ltd Glasgow

Contents

1. *Introduction*

> Change is a principle of life.
> All is flux; nothing stands still.[1]

Many changes, for instance evolutionary changes in the period before the emergence of man, have taken place independently of any human action. These would be regarded by those who believe in God as due to his agency alone, and by those who do not as automatic and inevitable. The appearance of man on the scene of history has meant that he is at any rate a partner in this process with the ability to influence the direction which it takes.[2] Changes then are no longer – if ever they were – simply external. Those who are involved in changes have some capacity for determining the direction they take, and all are affected by them.[3] This is as it should be, for without change there can be no growth or progress. But the assumption that every change is for the better, that progress is inevitable, too easily made a century ago, has been shattered by two world wars and their aftermath. Those who believe in God believe that every change for the better depends upon human co-operation with his initiative; and even unbelievers recognize that they cannot take place without enlightened and sustained human effort.

But life can never stand still. If changes are not for the better they will necessarily be for the worse.

> All that is human must be retrograde
> if it does not advance.[4]

In spite of spectacular achievements in the field of the natural sciences, in medicine and technology, there are many ominous signs to confirm the gloomy observation of the Victorian hymn writer, so uncharacteristic of the age in which he lived, that contemporary changes tend to decay.

> The culture of Europe has deteriorated visibly within the memory of many who are by no means the oldest among us. And we know, that whether education can foster and improve culture or not, it can surely adulterate and degrade it . . . we can assert with some confidence that our own period is one of decline; that the standards of culture are lower than they were fifty years ago; and that the evidences of decline are visible in every department of human activity.[5]

Subsequent developments have only confirmed the truth of these words written in 1946.

The contribution which men and women can make to a changing world depends upon the development of their individual talents and the motives which determine the exercise and use to which these are put. If human potentialities are not realized and used, individuals and society will be the poorer. In this connection education is obviously important though it is not a panacea. When men's primary motive is self-interest their contribution to the changing world is unlikely — except incidentally — to serve the well-being and culture of society at large. When, more rarely, their dominant motive is the disinterested service of God and other people, their contribution is likely to be constructive and far-reaching.

But the contribution which men and women make to

the growth and enrichment of the life and culture of their time depends also and largely upon their convictions and assumptions. A conviction represents a condition of being convinced, a settled persuasion that certain things are true, which influences and shapes ideals and conduct. The conviction of St Francis of Assisi that God is the Creator and Father of all led him to regard and treat all creatures as his brothers and sisters. It was because Columbus was convinced that there was a continent beyond the Atlantic that he could not rest until he had found it. Convictions are definite and clear-cut. They are likely to be characteristic of those who have been educated to use their minds, but they are neither confined to such persons nor always to be found in them.

Assumptions are suppositions, less clearly defined and thought out than convictions, and often unconsciously acquired and held. They are more common than convictions and form the basis of many of our attitudes and actions. We book a room for our holiday next summer on the assumption that we shall still then be alive, or seats at the cinema on the assumption that it will be showing the film advertised in the newspaper.

Our convictions and assumptions have to be regularly re-examined in the light of our experience and the changing life of the world around us. After Galileo, men who had taken it for granted that the earth was flat and the centre of the universe had radically to change their thinking in the light of his demonstration that this was not the case. The disciples of Christ had to revise their preconceived ideas about God, inherited from Judaism, in the light of their knowledge and experience of his Son, Jesus Christ. Unless our ideas keep pace with our experience we live in a fool's paradise in which theory and practice bear no relation whatsoever to one another.

Many of our dilemmas may be due to the schizophrenia which comes from the vain attempt to reconcile twentieth-century living with nineteenth-century assumptions to which, often unconsciously, we continue to cling.

Intellectual integrity and consistency are rare enough even among the few who have strong convictions; and most people do not. The attitudes and actions of the majority are based on assumptions which are often simply caught from other people (*popular* assumptions), and are rarely consciously defined, articulated or considered. If these assumptions (or convictions) are true they provide a firm foundation for living : if they are false they can lead only to retrogression and collapse.

Many popular and influential assumptions about life which are widely taken for granted and only occasionally questioned are certainly mistaken. Some of them will be considered in subsequent chapters. They are not wholly false in that they contain some truth. They are true as far as they go, but they do not go far enough. It is precisely their incompleteness which makes them dangerously inadequate, for assumptions which are partially true possess an authority which complete and patent falsity can never command. Fundamental truths are always complex and many-sided; they defy superficial explanation and can only be stated in paradoxical terms. A paradox requires us to hold together in tension statements which are apparently contradictory or absurd, yet contain elements which are essentially complementary and true : it makes demands upon our minds with which we are reluctant to grapple. We prefer to take refuge in misleading oversimplification and to see matters in terms of *either – or* rather than *both – and,* and to settle for a shallow judgement on people or things, *as nothing but* rather than *both – and*. Only those who have no aesthetic appreciation are likely to maintain that a violin recital is nothing but 'the drawing of the tail of a dead horse across the guts of a dead cat'; and even a thorough-going materialist would be unlikely to assert that a human being is nothing but the sum of his physical constituents which, it has been said, amount to nine-tenths water and one-tenth salts. But many would assume that a person is either body or spirit but cannot be both; or that Jesus Christ cannot be God and man and is, in all probability, nothing but a man.

The everyday assumptions we make about mundane and minor matters – such as when the bank closes – can only, if they are mistaken, cause us some inconvenience. But assumptions which influence our thinking and action in relation to such fundamental matters as the reality of God, the structure of the universe or the nature of man must have disastrous consequences if they are false or only partially true. Life based on false assumptions is not only misunderstood and misinterpreted but impoverished in all its departments because those assumptions are necessarily reductionist in their nature and effects. To assume that a man is nothing but an animal, an individual or a social creature reduces his humanity, limits his capacity for personal fulfilment and for serving society, and obscures both the point of his present existence and his future destiny. When life is so stunted real growth is impossible and decay must set in.

The changes which tend to decay can be arrested and reversed if we are prepared to begin by identifying and critically examining widely held and rarely questioned basic assumptions about life, in order to be in a better position to correct their errors and to supply their defects. But the exposure of error is of little use unless it is accompanied by some indication of where truth is to be found. This book is written in the conviction that truth can be found only in God who in the life and teaching of Christ has revealed it to men in terms which they can understand. Every human conviction and assumption has to be measured against the standard of him who claims to be the Way, the Truth and the Life.

> Every one then who hears these words of mine and does them will be like a wise man who built his house upon the rock; and the rain fell, and the floods came, and the winds blew and beat upon that house, but it did not fall, because it had been founded on the rock. And every one who hears these words of mine and does not do them will be like a foolish man who built his house upon the sand; and the rain fell, and the floods came, and the winds blew and beat against that house, and it fell; and great was the fall of it.[6]

All that follows is an extended commentary on this familiar parable.

2. *The Cult of the Contemporary*

A conspicuous characteristic of many people today is their phrenetic preoccupation with the present. Life is nothing but today. They pay little or no attention to the past, of which we can know something, or to the future, of which we can know nothing. Both are regarded as equally irrelevant. As C. S. Lewis once remarked (in one of his lectures), it is an assumption made by men of the machine age that 'the new is better.' In a limited sense this may perhaps be true. Planned obsolescence makes it probable that a 1974 motor-car may be better than its 1972 predecessor. But this does not necessarily mean that either is intrinsically better – whatever that word may denote in this context – at any rate in durability and workmanship than a 1930 model which is still on the road. And even if it were true of manufactured goods that the new is better, it would not necessarily follow that this is true of anything else.

This assumption is held equally strongly and uncritically in the space age. There are many today who worship anything new precisely and only because it *is* new. Like the Athenians to whom St Paul tried with little success to commend the Gospel, they 'spent their time in nothing except telling or hearing something new'.[1] Newness is all. Intrinsic goodness, truth or beauty are neither considered nor regarded as of any importance. The only criterion – or cliché – of those who assume that the new is better is relevance.

Religion, like anything else which has its roots in the

past, is dismissed as irrelevant. But, as Martin Luther truly and succinctly remarked, 'If man will not have God he will have an idol.' Idols proliferate in an inventive age, and those who worship modernity for its own sake worship not one idol but many. Some are as tangible as the figures of wood and stone before which our forebears bowed the knee : the gleaming motor-car, the pretentious mansion or maisonette, the colour television set, the trendy clothes and the countless other visible symbols of status, affluence or culture which dominate and subjugate us. More subtle and insidious are the intangible idols which compete for our allegiance, the prevailing fads in religion, music, art or health.

One error leads to another, and the assumption that the new is better produces a corollary that is equally untrue. This is that we have nothing to learn from the past, a tacit endorsement of Henry Ford's notorious and contemptuous dismissal of history as bunk. Those who are obsessed by the present are convinced that their own first-hand experience alone possesses authority and validity. In consequence they draw a false distinction between experience and history. They do not recognize that history represents the accumulated experience of past generations confronted by situations which are often in their essential features very similar to those which face us today. The traditions we inherit, if we will heed them, can assist us in solving problems which are not peculiarly our own; and we cannot afford to dismiss as irrelevant the lessons of the past. The present is but a fragment of history, and our contemporary experience can only be understood and evaluated in the light of that of those who have lived before us. Only arrogance or complacency can blind us to the truth that we are pygmies who stand on the shoulders of giants. We are not confronted here by alternative options. This is not a matter of choosing between *either* present *or* past experience, but of paying attention to the lessons we can learn from both. Whether we find in history 'a cordial for drooping spirits'[2] or 'a purge for complacent optimism',[3] we ignore it at our peril.

Excessive preoccupation with the present also leads to neglect of the future. This, if more understandable, is no less misguided than contempt for the past. It is understandable because in a world which is changing as rapidly as ours it is harder than ever to anticipate the course of future developments. Prospects and possibilities are almost unlimited, and many of them give us grounds for foreboding. Deep-rooted fears for the future explain but do not excuse the shortsightedness which characterizes the attitudes and actions of men and nations. The policies often pursued by many governments appear to be cynically designed to defer action on apparently insoluble problems and to bequeath them to their successors. When those in high places seem to be principally concerned with passing the buck, it is not surprising that people in general follow their bad example. Principles of morality are discarded as being as irrelevant as history. Each individual reacts to every ethical situation as it arises in a manner which appears most likely to justify his own wishes and interests. Actions are governed not by principle but by impulse; and when some justification for conduct is offered, the authority of conscience is nullified by the fact that it is rarely educated or informed.

In practice many see as their main object in life the indefinite postponement of unpleasant possibilities; and their actions are determined in relation to the immediate results which they will probably produce without any regard for their remoter implications or consequences.[4] They live by the old pagan slogan, 'Eat, drink and be merry, for tomorrow we die', and the devil take our successors. Ideals and principles are repudiated, and selfish and shortsighted pragmatism reigns.

Another disturbing feature of modern life is the problem of communication. This is not a new problem, for people of different languages, cultures, occupations and ages have never found it easy to understand and communicate with one another. But it is a problem which for various reasons is today steadily becoming greater and more difficult to resolve. One alarming instance is the growth of the generation gap, and to this the exaggerated importance attached to the present at the expense of the past and the future appears to have contributed. It is natural that it should be younger people who are generally – but by no means invariably – more prone than their elders to infection by the cult of the contemporary. Parents have lived through a past of which their children have little knowledge and no direct experience. It is true that the experience, assumptions, conventions and tastes of succeeding generations must always to some extent differ. But in an age of rapid transition the gulfs between different groups, including that between one generation and the next, become steadily wider and deeper. Parents and children are like parties on opposite banks of a river in spate whose attempts to shout to one another across it are drowned by the roar of the waters between them. The problem of communication is a matter to which we must later return.

The influence of the cult of the contemporary is apparent in many departments of human life and thought, including philosophy. Here it finds expression in *existentialism,* 'the most characteristic product of western thought in the twentieth century'.[5] Existentialism 'asserts the absolute meaninglessness of the historical process, and immures men within the given situation at any given time'.[6] The imprisonment and isolation of men within the present which this philosophy involves explains the spirit of futility and despair which characterizes its disciples. If we are to discern any pattern or purpose in life it is to history that we must look for clues. Sören Kierkegaard, the nineteenth-century father of modern existentialism, defined the absurd as that which cannot be fitted into the pattern : but if the source from which evidence of the pattern might be derived is dismissed as irrelevant, the search for it is simply a wild-goose chase. The only logical conclusion to be drawn is that of Sartre, who maintains that life has no pattern, meaning or purpose whatsoever. The patron and exemplar of existentialists is not Christ but Sisyphus, who was condemned in the underworld to roll a huge boulder up a steep hill; but before it reached the top it always rolled back to the bottom, and Sisyphus had to start all over again. Existentialism is, however, certainly a philosophy of personal being. Man is unique; and because he possesses remarkable faculties and potentialities he is reluctant to acknowledge and accept the ultimate meaninglessness of his endeavours and existence. The anxiety by which he is haunted is due to the conflict which arises between his desire to believe that his life has some meaning, and his conviction that this is simply wishful thinking. The dilemma of existentialism is personified in Albert Camus, who longed for a faith to live by, for which the logic of his thought could find neither place nor justification. His unnecessary death in a motor-car accident was tragically consistent with the meaninglessness which he attributed to life.

Existentialism is essentially reductionist. It refuses to acknowledge – in effect it denies – the many-sidedness of man's nature, the scope and purpose of his potentialities, the validity of his aspirations and the object of his existence. It assumes that man is nothing but an individual, a lonely and ephemeral fragment of humanity. It ignores the social aspect and implications of his being, the solidarity of mankind which binds all men together in the bonds of natural interdependence.

It is perhaps worth noticing in parenthesis that another philosophy which competes for the minds of contemporary men, although it too is atheistic, differs widely from existentialism in many other of its basic assumptions. Marxism too tends in various ways to reduce and dehumanize man, but it does not isolate him. It takes account not only of the present but also of the past and the future. It seeks to understand man's present condition in the light of his past, and to ameliorate it by learning the lessons of history. It looks too with apocalyptic zeal and assurance to the future for the realization of the final destiny of mankind. Marxism reduces man not by isolating him but by treating him as nothing but a social creature. The individual is submerged beneath the sea of humanity. Persons are sacrificed to society.

No system of thought, even if it derives from divine revelation, can entirely escape the influence of the trends and tendencies which constitute and shape the climate of opinion, and Christian theology is no exception. The powerful influence of the cult of the contemporary can be clearly discerned in the *new theology*.[7]

Its exponents are rightly concerned that the Gospel should be effectively proclaimed in terms which modern man can understand. They have not however succeeded in avoiding the danger of achieving intelligibility at the cost of truth, and it is a diminished Gospel which they proclaim. They lay such stress upon God's presence in the world, events and people of today that they obscure – or even by implication deny – his eternal reality as Creator and Lord of the universe, which wholly depends upon him, as he can never depend upon it. Their exclusive insistence on God's presence here and now further leads them to neglect, if not entirely to ignore, God's involvement in the past and his purposes for the future. They share with the contemporary world a diminished awareness not only of the dimension of eternity but of the significance of time, and too readily identify the spirit of the age with the Holy Spirit of God. If the vocation of the Christian theologian is that of 'relating the revealed datum of Christian truth, final, absolute and fundamentally permanent . . . to the essentially incomplete, relative and constantly changing intellectual framework of the world in which he lives',[8] the new theologians have misunderstood it. They plainly do less than justice to the fullness of the Gospel of Jesus Christ, who is 'the same yesterday and today and for ever'.[9]

In the person of Christ not only the present but time in all its dimensions past, present and future is set in the context of eternity. The Incarnation is the embodiment of the eternal. He who is eternally God became man, the man Jesus of Nazareth. This is the significance of the tremendous affirmation by which Christ identified himself with God who revealed himself to Moses in the burning bush, words which in their blindness his enemies could only interpret as blasphemy:

> Before Abraham was, I am.[10]

Christ's birth is the focal point of history, and the moment when BC became AD is decisive for mankind and the world.

> In the beginning was the Word, and the Word was with God, and the Word was God . . . And the Word became flesh and dwelt among us, full of grace and truth.[11]

By becoming man Christ identified himself with all men in every age : by becoming man at a particular moment of time he revealed the significance, unity and continuity of the whole time process. His person and work can only be understood in the light of the past; and at the very outset of his early ministry he proclaimed that in him the promises and prophecies of the Old Testament are fulfilled :

> Today this scripture has been fulfilled in your hearing.[12]

He is the Messiah to whose coming the Jews had for centuries looked forward, and although he is unlike the sort of saviour they had expected, his identity and mission could only be understood in terms of Israel's history. No more than they can we today begin to understand the New Testament if we ignore the Old, in which Christ's coming was foreshadowed and which informed his thought and permeated his teaching.[13]

> Think not that I have come to abolish the law and the prophets; I have come not to abolish them but to fulfil them.[14]

But history never repeats itself exactly; and present situations with the demands they make are not precisely the same as those by which previous generations were confronted. Christ recognized that fulfilment requires much more than the tacit and uncritical acquiescence which his opponents – the respectable religious people of his day – gave to traditional interpretations. This is exemplified by his attitude to Sabbath observance :

> The sabbath was made for man, not man for the sabbath; so the Son of man is lord even of the sabbath.[15]

He suffers from no obsession with the past for its own sake, and never makes attention to its lessons a pretext for ignoring the demands of the present but rather an aid to understanding and responding to them. He is always ready to give himself completely to the people and situations which immediately confront him, without regard to his own convenience or to other urgent claims upon him. He interrupts his sermon in the synagogue at Capernaum to heal a lunatic[16]; postpones his supper at the end of an exhausting day in order to heal Simon's mother-in-law and the other invalids who sought him out[17]; and stops on his way to the death-bed of Jairus' daughter to attend to a woman whose chronic complaint was far less serious.[18] So completely did he put himself at the disposal of those who needed him, without regard for himself, that his family and friends thought him mad.[19] And even as he faced the immediacy and suffering of his own execution he thought not of his own predicament but of the needs of those who shared responsibility for it. He restored Malchus' ear, sought to resolve Pilate's perplexity and prayed that his executioners might be forgiven.[20]

As the present has its roots in the past so also it has significance for the future. Christ's injunction against anxiety about tomorrow's needs does not mean that we are to be completely irresponsible in the ordering of our affairs, or that we should ignore the implications of our actions today.[21] He repeatedly insists upon the far-reaching and irrevocable consequences of the use men make of their talents and present opportunities. The shortsightedness of the rich fool, preoccupied with his own material self-interest, which blinds him to the precariousness of human life and his own mortality, brings its own fearful reward.[22] Those who have had the chance of knowing and responding to God's will call down upon themselves a condemnation more severe than those who have had no such opportunity.[23] The foolish young women who took no spare oil for their lamps missed a unique opportunity which would never recur.[24] The pusillanimous sluggard who made no use of his talent forfeited for ever the destiny which might have been his. He shared with the rich man the condemnation of all those who reject opportunities for serving and helping others :

> They will go away into eternal punishment, but the righteous into eternal life.[25]

The Gospels make it clear that our understanding, not only of our individual destiny but of the whole universe, depends upon our readiness to see the present in the light of the future as well as the past. The eschatological passages[26] which deal with death, judgement, Heaven and hell (and reproduce ideas, language and images found in similar passages in the Old Testament) are difficult and disturbing. It is significant that the new theologians pay little or no attention to them. But these passages are *there*. However hard we may find them, we can neither ignore them nor explain them away.

The cult of the contemporary emphasizes an important fact of life, that we must take seriously the situation in which we find ourselves today, the opportunities it offers and the demands it makes. This is a truth so obvious that it should not need to be stated. But escapism in one form or another is a powerful temptation which few are spared, and to which religious people including Christians are particularly prone. It is only too easy to take refuge in 'religious duties', to prostitute worship by using it to enable us to evade less congenial occupations, instead of seeing it as the primary, self-authenticating activity which inspires and sanctifies everything else that we do. Or again, we can run away from our present responsibilities by wasting our time sentimentally hankering after the (supposedly) good old days or consoling ourselves with the prospect of 'pie in the sky when we die'.

We can find no warrant whatsoever in the Gospels for such self-indulgence. The example and teaching of Christ require us to use to the full the opportunities for serving God and men which each succeeding moment offers to us. St Paul in his well-known exhortation to the Colossians is equally insistent on this point :

> Whatever your task, work heartily, as serving the Lord and not men, knowing that from the Lord you will receive the inheritance as your reward.[27]

And he supports his warning to the Thessalonians against making their expectations an excuse for doing nothing by reminding them of the example he has set them:

> Now we command you, brethern, in the name of our Lord Jesus Christ, that you keep away from any brother who is living in idleness and not in accord with the tradition that you received from us. For you yourselves know how you ought to imitate us; we were not idle when we were with you.[28]

The cult of the contemporary is mistaken in suggesting that nothing matters but the present, that all else is irrelevant. It is a mistake which reduces men by limiting their ability to understand themselves – their antecedents, their potentialities and their destiny – as well as the world to which they belong. The solidarity of mankind, men's relationship with one another and with the world of which they are an integral part, is revealed in the natural order which God has created and, supremely, in the Incarnation of his Son. Each moment is not a fragment but a sacrament,[29] a God-given opportunity to be used in his service and so to become a tiny contribution to the ultimate fulfilment of his all-embracing purpose for ourselves and for his world.

3. *Secularism*

Secularism is based on the supposition that the physical universe is the only reality and contains within itself both its own inbuilt mechanism and all clues to its meaning. All things, including the most developed forms of life, can be explained in purely material terms. Even the unique properties of man – his capacity to think, to choose, to appreciate and to love – derive from and are entirely shaped by his own physical nature and his environment. His ability to make moral decisions is an illusion because his behaviour is completely conditioned by material factors. His spiritual attributes and aspirations are nothing more than figments of his imagination stimulated by wishful thinking. The basic false assumption of secularism is that nothing but the visible universe is real. The world is all : it is self-sufficient, self-supporting and self-perpetuating. There is no creator.

Secularization has been well described as 'the transition from beliefs and activities and institutions presupposing beliefs of a traditional Christian kind to beliefs and activities and institutions of an atheistic kind'.[1] This is a process which continues steadily to penetrate every department of modern life and has a profound effect upon its direction and organization. The dangers of secularism and the assumption upon which it is based are still further increased by another assumption, equally widespread and false – that our culture is still distinctively and recognizably Christian. The lazy equation of the western way of life with Christian civilization shows that many are completely unaware of the scale and rapidity of the transition from a Christian to a post-Christian era. For those who have eyes to see the evidence that we live in a secular age is overwhelming.

Yet, like other people, even the avowed disciples of secularism are thinking animals, and they find it difficult to be satisfied with the absolute materialism and rigid determinism to which the logic of their presuppositions commits them. In practice they seek some principle or spirit of coherence and intelligibility within the universe which they deny can be sought outside it. If a creator is excluded, some god-substitute must be sought within the framework of creation; and secularism finds 'religious' expression in some form of immanentism or pantheism – the perennial philosophy.

> Men are not content to be merely kind and clever within the limits of a concrete situation. They aspire to relate their actions, and the thoughts and feelings accompanying those actions, to general principles and a philosophy on the cosmic scale.[2]

Man's deep-rooted yearning for contact with the divine cannot be repressed even by those who are unable to find any rational justification for it : nor can this instinct be satisfied by his efforts to find communion with a spirit which is merely immanent in this world and has no independent existence. The inadequacy of such a limited conception is reflected by the widespread interest in the Christian mystics of both the Huxley brothers. Julian Huxley makes extensive quotations from them, and Aldous claims to share their experience as a result of his experiments with mescalin.[3] The popularity of eastern mysticism, itself essentially pantheistic, may well be explained, at least in part, by the inability of a thorough-going secularism to satisfy basic human aspirations and needs.

If existentialism is one of the characteristic products of the twentieth century, logical positivism is another and reflects its secular assumptions. Positivism in all its forms is distinguished by its wholesale rejection of thought-forms which claim to deal with anything other than physical realities. In its more recent developments it asserts the impossibility of rational discussion of the subjects dealt with by metaphysics or theology because they cannot be demonstrated to be true or false by experience. Religious language is simply meaningless, entirely devoid of significance or validity. Even to attempt to talk of God is non-sense.[4]

Those who reject God know nothing greater than themselves, and secularism makes man at least a demi-god. Since it regards him as the product of his history, heredity and environment, it cannot claim that man is completely self-made. But it admits few if any limits upon his unaided ability to triumph over all life's challenges. What man makes of himself depends entirely upon himself. It is a curious mixture of self-confidence and fatalism.

> Under the bludgeonings of chance
> My head is bloody, but unbowed . . .
> It matters not how strait the gate,
> How charged with punishments the scroll,
> I am the master of my fate :
> I am the captain of my soul.[5]

It is surprising that the self-confidence expressed by the Victorian poet, although shaken, has not been entirely destroyed by two world wars and their aftermath. This is due not only to the fact that our memories are short, but far more to the spectacular success of natural scientists in exploiting the physical resources of the world for human purposes. These are the supermen whom we reverence and before whose achievements we are lost in wonder. They are the priests of the secular order who have replaced religious men in the hierarchy of mankind :

> Secularization in the modern world . . . contains an implication that the sacred is irrelevant. Not only are priests and scientists distinguished but the scientist is held to be important, the priest unimportant.[6]

Human achievements are designed to benefit not only the few who are primarily responsible for them, but the whole human race. The fact that in practice they are often used for destructive purposes raises questions to which secularism can give no convincing answers. Indeed the conditions which make these achievements possible promote deeper divisions; for the price which has to be paid for advance in any department of human knowledge is that of intensive specialization. If a child is eventually to make his mark in the natural sciences or any other discipline and to compete in the modern world, he must from an early age devote all his energies to studying one subject to the virtual exclusion of all others. The faith which secularism places in man means that it regards education as a panacea. But early and exclusive specialization in any single subject cannot really *educate*; it may produce brilliant freaks, but not complete people. The function of education is to elicit and develop *all* the latent gifts and potentialities which an individual possesses, to produce balanced and integrated persons who are all of a piece. Since the high degree of specialization which competitive life in secular society demands breeds people qualified only in one subject, they lose their capacity for understanding those trained in any discipline but their own. Every trade or profession produces its own jargon intelligible only to insiders and beyond the understanding of everyone else. Secularism is responsible not only for corrupting education by narrowing its range, but also for further aggravating the problem of communication by the occupation-gap which it creates.

There are only two possible alternative motives or incentives for action which can be offered by a system which affirms that this world alone is real : they are service or self-interest.

Many secular humanists are people of high principles and ideals. They sincerely desire to devote all their energies and abilities to promoting the (material) well-being of mankind; and their selflessness is both a challenge and a reproach to many Christians. Such dedication and idealism is by no means confined to doctors, in whom, perhaps, it is most apparent. Edward Teller, the nuclear physicist, at great personal cost abandoned his research when he saw clearly that it would be used not to promote but to destroy human life, and he is far from standing alone. If high ideals were enough the validity of secular humanism which dispenses with God might well appear to be vindicated. But history and present experience make it plainly apparent that much more than good intentions is necessary, and confirm the truth of Mr Gladstone's conviction 'that secular motives are not adequate either to propel or to restrain the children of our race'. Even conspicuous devotion to the service of others cannot of itself generate the power which its translation into practice requires. Liberty, equality and fraternity are noble ideals. But the French, Russian and countless other revolutions quickly degenerated into bloodbaths. The devotion and integrity of Tellers are submerged by the selfishness of others.

It is a fundamental weakness of secular humanism that it consistently fails to recognize the power and pervasiveness of human selfishness or acquisitiveness, and assumes that it can be eradicated simply by programmes of social improvement. As a character in a novel of one of the latest victims of Russian 'idealism' remarks with pregnant simplicity: 'There were greedy people *before* the bourgeoisie and there'll be greedy people *after* the bourgeoisie.' The dominant motive of those who belong to a secular society will always be self-interest, and nations and individuals are concerned above all else with securing and extending their own material interests : and it is the clash between competing interests which leads inevitably to every kind of human conflict, to world and civil wars, to strikes and class struggles, and to domestic quarrels.

Conduct determined by self-interest cannot but destroy : and as men compete ever more fiercely for the world's resources and continue to develop and exploit them for their own purposes, the prospect and possibility of universal self-destruction is terrifying indeed :

> And appetite, an universal wolf,
> So doubly seconded with will and power,
> Must make perforce an universal prey, ·
> And last eat up himself.[8]

Secularism reduces man to the sum of his physical constituents. Its object is 'desacralization, the enthronement of truncated man';[9] for any attempt to put man in God's place defeats its own ends.[10] It is impossible for human beings to grow up into their full stature within the narrow framework of a life based on the assumption that both they and the world are composed of merely material elements. Nor do we find it easy to believe that our unique capacities for thought, love and appreciation of moral and aesthetic values can be explained simply in terms of purely chemical reactions, or that all our behaviour is absolutely predetermined by immutable conditions.

It is unnecessary to be a Christian in order to recognize the inadequacy of secularism and the gaps in human life and experience which it can make no convincing attempt to fill. There are natural scientists who make no pretence of believing in God and yet peer beyond the horizon of their own discipline to the mystery which surrounds the physical universe, whose secrets they know they can only begin to probe : and there are agnostic artists who realize that their finest work represents but a shadow of the vision of beauty which they glimpse but try in vain to reproduce. Such men are aware, even if they cannot explain it, that their inspiration and abilities derive from more than merely physical sources.

G. Kepes' *The New Landscape* – one of the most remarkable books on art in recent years. It opens up a world as unattainable to the limited range of our senses – the 'narrow biological filter of perception' – as light and colour are unattainable to the blind. 'Of the total stimuli flooding the world with potential messages, the visible and audible ranges accessible to our bodies represent a tiny segment.'[11]

Man cannot live and grow in the strait-jacket of secularism.

Christian theology has not escaped the impact and influence of secularism and its assumptions. Theologians upon whom this impact has been most severe have gone so far as to cut off the branch upon which they are sitting by claiming that God, whom the world rejects, is dead. In spite of their efforts to preserve theology they have killed it too by making it meaningless. Others equally concerned to relate theology to secular life and thought, but unable to endorse such an extreme position, try to preserve God by identifying him with his world. God is reduced to the 'ground of our being', the principle which resides in creation and supports and sustains every creature in life. They attempt, however, to preserve God's reality at the price of depriving him of his independence and status as creator. Nor is there anything personal about the nature of such a deity; and the theology which expounds this manner of thinking is in fact not theistic but pantheistic.[12] Like the avowed secularists, whose thought they try to accommodate, they give God's pre-eminence to human beings and assert erroneously that man has 'come of age'.

The extent to which Christianity has become secularized is demonstrated not only by these trends in theology but also in popular understanding of its character and principles and of its practical implications for Christian living. We are encouraged to acquiesce in the secular view that the horizontal is the only dimension of life, that we fulfil all our responsibilities to God as well as men by doing our duty to our fellows. Worship and prayer are at best harmless diversions, and at worst easy escapes from our real obligations. Personal relationships and mutual service are the only real forms of prayer. Councils of Churches, congregations and individual Christians devote *all* their energies and resources to social service and the relief of the victims of war, poverty, injustice or discrimination. Their claim that preoccupation with such activities constitutes the whole of Christianity gains credibility from the fact that they are certainly an indispensable part of it which professing Christians have frequently ignored and neglected. Feelings of guilt in respect of our blatant failures in care and concern for other people give added force to the claims which the social gospel makes upon us.

> If any one says, 'I love God,' and hates his brother, he is a liar.

It is a warning that we forget at our peril; and we hate our brother not only by active animosity but also by passive neglect. But it is significant that St John continues:

> And this commandment we have from him, *that he who loves God* should love his brother also.[18]

Love for our brother is a necessary extension and demonstration of our love for God. But all love derives from God who *is* love; and all human love can only begin in loving him for his own sake. The command to love our neighbour is the second, not the first, part of the great commandment. There is much more to the Gospel of Christ than the social gospel.

When Christ became man he identified himself with humanity and affirmed the essential goodness of the material universe as God's creation. Man's abuse of his freedom which involved the world in his own corruption could not entirely destroy its intrinsic goodness. If *total* corruption had been the consequence, it is open to question whether God's Son could have become flesh. The Incarnation initiates the re-creation of God's children and his world in all its aspects, and restores to the whole created order the possibility of its growth into that perfection for which God created and designed it.

> For the creation was subjected to futility, not of its own will but by the will of him who subjected it in hope; because the creation itself will be set free from its bondage to decay and obtain the glorious liberty of the children of God.[14]

It is significant that two of the earliest and related heresies, whose seeds can be discerned in the New Testament itself, denied both the reality of the Incarnation and the goodness of matter. One claimed that Christ's humanity is an illusion, the other that all matter is intrinsically evil – the creation not of God but of an intrusive and wicked demi-god :

> By this you know the Spirit of God : every spirit which confesses that Jesus Christ has come in the flesh is of God, and every spirit which does not confess Jesus is not of God.
> For many deceivers have gone out into the world, men who will not acknowledge the coming of Jesus Christ in the flesh.[15]

It was a real human life which Christ lived. He did not stand aloof from human joys and sorrows but shared

to the full the everyday life of his contemporaries. Born
of a human mother, he was brought up with his relatives
in the home of a village craftsman. The very ordinari-
ness of his childhood was early made a pretext for re-
jecting him :

> 'Is not this the carpenter, the son of Mary and brother
> of James and Joses and Judas and Simon, and are not
> his sisters here with us?' And they took offence at
> him.[16]

At the beginning of his ministry Christ chose
twelve men to be his constant companions and set much
store by their company, not least in the moments when
they failed and deserted him.[17] He included women as
well as men among his friends, and during the last week
of his earthly life he found refuge and peace at the end
of each day in the hospitality of the home at Bethany.
He entered fully into social occasions, was never
particular about the kind of company he kept and reminded those who criticized his lack of discrimination
that they could not have it both ways :

> For John came neither eating nor drinking, and they
> say, 'He has a demon'; the Son of man came eating
> and drinking, and they say, 'Behold, a glutton and a
> drunkard, a friend of tax collectors and sinners!'[18]

One at least of the disreputable characters whom he
accosted in the street, and whose hospitality he enjoyed,
became a faithful disciple.[19]

Although himself unmarried Christ with his disciples
attended a village wedding, and by his first recorded
sign saved the host from embarrassment and the

occasion from disaster.[20] He was concerned to supply the material as well as the spiritual needs of the crowd who had listened to him all day, and refused to allow them to be sent away without food.[21]

Christ knew that men are human beings and not angels, that they have bodies as well as souls. Nor did he ever forget that they have souls as well as bodies. Those who sought healing for their diseases were given first absolution from their sins, to the scandal of the by-standers:

When Jesus saw their faith, he said to the paralytic, 'My son, your sins are forgiven.' Now some of the scribes were sitting there, questioning in their hearts, 'Why does this man speak thus? It is blasphemy! Who can forgive sins but God alone?' Jesus . . . said to them, '. . . that you may know that the Son of man has authority on earth to forgive sins' – he said to the paralytic – 'I say to you, rise, take up your pallet, and go home.'[22]

The Incarnation, 'the supreme sacrament', points to the sacramentality of the whole universe. There is much more to man and the world than meets the eye. God the Creator is present and active in all his creatures, and men, the crown of creation, are his children made in his image. But God is not *only* in his world and cannot be identified with it. God is independent of his creation. Transcendent as well as immanent he exists over against the universe which he has created and, by his indwelling, ceaselessly sustains. But the God revealed by Christ is no impersonal first cause or life force. He is Father, the first person of the three who compose the mysterious unity of Godhead. Christ's relationship to the Father in the Spirit is rooted in eternity :

> In the beginning was the Word, and the Word was with God, and the Word was God.[23]

It remains the key relationship of his earthly life and ministry. It is in obedience to the Father that he came into the world – in the Father's name consistently to do the Father's will. It is to the Father that he returns when the Father's work has been perfectly accomplished. It is to the Father that he constantly prays and teaches us to pray.[24] It is the primary claim of this relationship which draws him apart, even from the insistent claims and needs of the crowds who throng him, in order that his unbroken and unbreakable communion with the Father may be constantly sustained. And Christ demonstrates that worship must always have first claim, not only upon our time but upon our resources, by commending the action of Mary of Bethany, who expressed her love by conduct which seemed to be extravagant and irresponsible :

> 'Why was this ointment not sold for three hundred denarii and given to the poor?' . . . Jesus said, 'Let her alone . . . The poor you always have with you, but you do not always have me.'[25]

Christ came to proclaim the good news of the kingdom of God, but this was not the earthly kingdom of popular expectation. The kingdom he came to inaugurate in this world could only be finally and fully established beyond the bounds of space and time :

'My kingship is not of this world.'[26]

It is within the perspective of eternity that he teaches us to pray :

> Thy kingdom come,
> Thy will be done,
> On earth as it is in Heaven.[27]

This, too, is the context in which he sets the institution of the Eucharist :

> '. . . I tell you that from now on I shall not drink of the fruit of the vine until the kingdom of God comes.'[28]

Here in the Upper Room on the night before he died Christ's concern for the salvation of men, their souls and their bodies, is epitomized and sacramentalized. Here he makes it clear that when we pray as he taught us,

> Give us this day our daily bread,

we are asking for far more than our bodily sustenance. In the Eucharist we are enabled to see, as did St John, the deep significance of the feeding of the multitude.[29] The bread and the wine which Christ blessed and gave to his first disciples were for them – and are for us – the food of immortality.

Secularism affirms an important truth which must be taken seriously, that this world *matters*. It is a truth of which Christians need constantly to be reminded. We easily make the mistake of supposing that material things are unimportant, irrelevant or even evil. God's revelation in Christ of himself and of the nature of men and the universe gives no warrant whatsoever for such a false supposition. Its victims, whether they know it or not, are heretics and not Christians. But secularism has grasped only part of the truth, and its basic assumption is so inadequate as to be entirely misleading. It is Christ who reveals the whole truth, that God is our Father, that the universe is his creation, and that all men are his children, with souls as well as bodies, who are destined by his loving design, not only for brief existence in this world, but for eternal life in his kingdom.

4. *The Flight From Reason*

Future historians looking back on the twentieth century may, with some justification and in spite of its achievements, label it the Age of Unreason. The massive advances in many fields of human knowledge have been made by the few; the attitudes and activities of the many are characterized not by reason but by irrationalism. Although opportunities for gaining some sort of education have been extended to those who previously had none, most people have never really learned to develop and use their mental faculties; others have applied them only to matters which belong to their own specialist field, and in other respects put their minds into cold storage. Sir Arthur Conan Doyle, for example, was a remarkable novelist, a competent doctor, but a negligible theologian. Most people act most of the time entirely on impulse without any regard to the claims of reason.

The mind of man is one of his distinctive attributes, designed, in conjunction with his will, to guide and control the activities for which his emotions provide the motive force but not the direction. Our emotions are the necessary servants of these other faculties. But good servants, if they forget their place and usurp functions which do not belong to them, become bad masters. It is characteristic of our time that to a great extent our minds have been submerged by our instincts and emotions, which have become the potent and dangerous determinants of our behaviour. People who are dominated by their feelings lose any capacity for consistent action, and their behaviour is capricious and unpredictable. They live their lives from moment to moment in response to every passing whim. Their basic false assumption is that mind is unimportant, that what anyone thinks is immaterial and irrelevant. Convictions have no meaning, and those who have none of their own can neither understand nor respect those of other people. The empty mind is identified with the open mind. And by denying reason its proper place and function we exclude one of the essential elements in human nature which distinguishes us from the animals:

> O judgement! thou art fled to brutish beasts,
> And men have lost their reason.[1]

The widespread influence of irrationalism is seen in many departments of contemporary life.

We can see it in the impoverishment and prostitution of language. Words are the most convenient and effective symbols we have for framing, articulating and communicating our thoughts. The proper use of words is a condition of rational discourse between human beings. Such discourse is only possible so long as every word has its own distinct, defined and generally accepted meaning. Although words necessarily acquire emotional overtones and associations, they are designed primarily as means of communicating thoughts and ideas. Today, however, words are increasingly used without regard for their meaning, in order to promote purely emotional reactions. Texts are quoted out of context, catchwords are unthinkingly bandied about, and slogans which could not survive critical consideration are employed to arouse our passions or to batter us into acquiescence by sheer force of repetition. Public speeches are calculated not to convince but to whip up mass hysteria, and political, commercial and even religious propaganda is designed not to stimulate our minds but to anaesthetize them. Nor is this abuse of language confined to the market-place and the commercial broadcasting studio, where it is perhaps only to be expected : it extends to the corridors of power. Assemblies and parliaments, the traditional strongholds and custodians of responsible and rational debate, have become places where members are often principally concerned with stimulating animosities, scoring points or improving their own images. There can be no doubt that this deterioration at least contributes to the growing disenchantment with democratic institutions.[2] Talk at every level becomes progressively more empty, a hollow substitute for rational activity instead of its indispensable condition and source. And we become so dependent upon the incessant and mainly meaningless clamour which surrounds us that we are terrified of the silent reflection which thought requires. We speak before we think because we have lost the capacity for thought.

Other symbols of communication have suffered the same fate as words. Contemporary art and music rarely attempt to engage and satisfy our intellects, but only to assault our senses. Bach has been dethroned by the Beatles, and aesthetic appreciation is replaced by sentimentality.

It is a paradox that the prevalence of irrationalism coincides with the spread of popular education, that growth in literacy is accompanied by the popularity of the strip cartoon. This suggests that premature specialization is far from being the only defect of present methods and programmes of education. Student protests and demonstrations, for which there may be some justification, give grounds for disquiet not least because they are frequently expressed in extravagantly emotional terms. To refuse to allow visiting lecturers to state and explain their point of view, even if it is unpopular, is anything but rational. When even those who receive higher education and are potential future leaders sacrifice reason to emotion, we cannot be surprised when those who lack similar abilities and opportunities behave in the same manner. But the blame may rest less with the students than with the education they are offered. This is a matter which can only be, and is being, carefully considered by educationalists themselves. There is, however, one particular and alarming defect in some methods of popular education today : that is its superficiality.

Education cannot be confined to training in one discipline, nor is it an exclusively intellectual process. By definition and design it exists to draw out and develop every potentiality we possess, to promote the growth of the whole person. It is true that methods of education have often placed too much emphasis on intellectual training and too little on developing our other capacities and relationships. Today there is a danger that the pendulum will swing too far in the other direction. An influential tendency in contemporary education is so to stress growth in self-awareness and personal relationships as to neglect the importance of training the mind, and the discipline and application which this involves. This tendency is apparent in the techniques of group dynamics or leadership training which are now widely used for the purpose of secular and religious education. The primary purpose of their programmes is to deepen experience rather than knowledge, to promote emotional instead of intellectual maturity.

As trust in the group grows, people find a psychologically safe climate, and they begin to take off their masks and reduce their defensiveness. They begin to relate to one another at a deep level.

The caring community that develops helps one realize the potential of ordinary people and the wisdom of the group is often humbling and inspiring as people begin to reveal more of themselves and their basic problems. In such an atmosphere people are often encouraged to try new behaviours which they think may help their growth.[3]

There is obviously much that people can learn about themselves and one another by meeting in groups, and this is valuable. But this method has both limitations and dangers of which its exponents sometimes seem unaware. It is certainly not a type of training that should be recommended indiscriminately to all; it will benefit some but do real damage to others. It is very important that those in charge, the trainers, should be qualified for their responsibilities, and be able to draw the distinction between group training and group therapy, which demands expert knowledge and insight which they do not always possess. Above all it is essential to recognize that these methods are designed to deal with only one of the many aspects of education. Development in human relationships is an important part of the purpose of any educational programme, but not the whole of it. The intellectual content of group programmes is often slight. Members of a group can only bring to it what they themselves possess, and in many cases the intellectual contribution which they are capable of making is not considerable. A superficial consideration of a mass of often unrelated topics is a characteristic feature of groups which by design are given no fixed agenda; and each participant is encouraged to speak on any subject regardless of his or her competence to do so. Serious rational discussion is liable to go by default in a highly charged emotional atmosphere when a random group of people spend a limited period together at close quarters. There is a real danger that people meeting for a week under such conditions will use the occasion to form intimate relationships with one another as a means of escape from the much more exacting demands made upon them by their ordinary and enduring relationships in everyday life.[4]

Irrationalism has also contributed to the decline and erosion of moral standards. Ethics can have meaning only for those who have principles and convictions, who believe that certain things are good and should be done, and that other things are bad and should not. These are considerations which have neither meaning nor cogency for people who act habitually on impulse, as their feelings at any moment dictate, without regard for the consequences. This explains at least in part the upsurge of violence which is a sombre feature of our times. There have, of course, always been crimes of violence, for men suddenly and unexpectedly provoked do things in hot blood before they have time to think. But it is reasonable to expect that such things will occur less frequently in civilized societies when men have been trained and accustomed to reflect before they act. At a time, however, when rational consideration is out of fashion people make nonsense of the civilization which they claim by simply giving way to their every impulse. In these circumstances violence of every kind is bound to increase, and wholly irrational assaults without apparent motive constitute an increasing proportion of the escalating crime rate in many countries of the world.

Christianity has been influenced by irrationalism as by other trends and tendencies in contemporary life. Feelings have their proper and necessary place in religion, but here as elsewhere they are liable to get out of hand. The tendency to attach excessive importance to religious feelings and experience is nothing new; it became particularly pronounced in popular Christianity in the Middle Ages,[5] and was given added impetus at the Reformation. Catholicism and Eastern Orthodoxy have always emphasized the corporate and objective aspects of Christian faith, worship and life, by the importance they attach to the Church as Christ's Body, the creeds in which its faith is defined, and the liturgy as its characteristic activity. Protestantism reacted by stressing the subjective and individual aspects of Christianity; it attaches less importance to formularies of faith, and lays stress upon personal religion and free worship which provide greater scope for expressing emotions and feelings.

Both the objective and subjective elements are indispensable parts of the Christian faith: they are not mutually exclusive but complementary, and if either is sacrificed to the other Christianity is reduced and distorted. A proper ecumenism will hold both the Catholic and Protestant contributions in balance. But if Catholicism has in the past made inadequate provision for the place of religious emotion, Protestantism has provided too much, and has contributed to the exaggerated importance now attached to religious experience at the expense of theological truth.

Theology today is generally dismissed as the relatively harmless hobby of a few specialists, but wholly irrelevant to the circumstances and problems which ordinary men and women have to face in their daily lives. This is true even of the majority of sincere and practising Christians who leave the subject to their clergy, look for comfort not instruction from their sermons, and repeat the creeds without understanding either their meaning or their point. The decline of the established Churches is due in part to the fact that their formularies and liturgical worship fail to promote the pious feelings and experience which many of their members consider it the only function of religion to provide. The ranks of Pentecostalist and other revivalist sects are steadily swelled by those whose traditional practices did not give them what they sought; and Christians go the way of the world in seeking experience rather than truth as the goal of their earthly pilgrimage.

The rational element in religion is firmly entrenched in the Gospel and is implicit in the Incarnation. Christ is the Word, the Logos of God, and this has a significance far deeper than the English translation can provide. Logos signifies both language and reason, the intellect which enables us to think, as well as the words by which we try to give articulation and expression to our thoughts. The Word became flesh to reveal that rationality is one of the basic attributes of God, whose nature is in Christ communicated to us in the manner we can best understand. In Christ's earthly life and ministry, in this respect as in all others, the character of the Word of God is perfectly reproduced. Christ shares and expresses the emotions which all men possess, and without which he would have been less than fully human. He was moved by compassion for all who flocked to him, and by affection for the beloved disciple, for Martha and her family, and for the young man who volunteered for his service:

> Now Jesus loved Martha and her sister and Lazarus. And Jesus looking upon him loved him.[6]

The grave of Lazarus and the plight of Jerusalem reduced him to tears:

> Jesus wept. So the Jews said, 'See how he loved him!' . . . Then Jesus, deeply moved again, came to the tomb.
> And when he drew near and saw the city he wept over it.[7]

He agonized in Gethsemane.[8]

Yet Christ was at all times master of his feelings and never their slave. His life was dominated by the recognition that his Father had sent him into the world, and by his determination always to seek and do the Father's will without regard to his own feelings or the price of obedience. The steadfastness of Christ's purpose, his complete single-mindedness, caused perplexity and anxiety to his mother and Joseph, alarmed his disciples, and brought him to his Passion.

> 'Did you not know that I must be in my Father's house?' And they did not understand the saying which he spoke to them.
> 'I seek not my own will but the will of him who sent me.'
> And they were on the road, going up to Jerusalem, and Jesus was walking ahead of them; and they were

amazed, and those who followed were afraid.
And he said, 'Abba, Father, all things are possible to
thee; remove this cup from me; yet not what I will,
but what thou wilt.'[9]

In Christ the flesh was completely subdued to the
spirit, his own wishes and feelings to the Father's will,
which he made wholly his own. So too he consistently
refrained from making emotional appeals to the feelings
of others, nor would he allow them to make an
impetuous response to his call. On the contrary, he was
explicit in insisting that they should face the cost of
discipleship, which must involve their identification with
his own obedience to the Father. The youth who offered
his service was immediately confronted by a challenge
which he shrank from accepting :

And Jesus . . . said to him, 'You lack one thing; go,
sell what you have, and give it to the poor' . . . and
he went away sorrowful; for he had great possessions.[10]

A woman giving way to an emotional outburst was
brought down to earth by a reminder of the moral
responsibilities of the children of God :

A woman in the crowd raised her voice and said to
him, 'Blessed is the womb that bore you, and the
breasts that you sucked!' But he said, 'Blessed rather
are those who hear the word of God and keep it!'[11]

Simon Peter's characteristically impetuous declaration
of his undying loyalty is met by the warning that his
good intentions would fail when he was put to the test :

Peter declared to him, 'Though they all fall away because of you, I will never fall away.' Jesus said to him, 'Truly, I say to you, this very night, before the cock crows, you will deny me three times.'[12]

Mary Magdalene, carried away by her feelings when she met the risen Lord, is discouraged from indulging them and given a practical commission to carry out:

Jesus said to her, 'Do not hold me . . . but go to my brethren.'[13]

Christ well knew the danger of people being swept away by their feelings as a result of his presence, his miracles and his preaching; and he consistently refused to seek from men and women an emotional response which he knew to be an inadequate foundation for enduring loyalty and discipleship. The thrust of his teaching is directed primarily to the minds of his hearers in order that, through conviction of the truth that he is and proclaims, they might be brought to lasting commitment. This is made very clear by his parables, which are notable for their objectivity. They are framed not in the second person but in the third, and their appeal is invariably indirect:

'A sower went out to sow.'
'The kingdom of Heaven may be compared to a man who sowed good seed in his field.'
'The kingdom of Heaven is like a grain of mustard seed . . . like treasure hidden in a field . . . like a merchant in search of fine pearls . . . like a net.'[14]

Christ's methods of proclaiming the Gospel are very

different from those of many modern evangelists and preachers, who too readily obtrude their own personalities, seem more concerned to arouse an emotional response than to commend the Gospel, bring men rather to themselves than to Christ, and in consequence produce only ephemeral effects which often last no longer than the feelings they arouse.

The mind of man is not his only attribute, and any suggestion expressed or implied that he is nothing but a thinking creature is wholly untrue. To exalt our rational faculties at the expense of our wills and feelings is as dangerous as to subordinate them. The recognition of the primacy of our minds is not to deny the indispensable but subsidiary role which these other faculties have to play in our life and growth as human beings.

The human mind is no infallible guide. The range and scope of our rational faculties are very limited. Our thinking is only 'the thinnest possible film on the surface of a vast deep'.[15] In addition to their inherent limitations our minds share the corruption with which sin has tainted the whole of human nature, and so they fall easy victims to ideologies, rationalizations and other errors. But although we realize the limitations and defects of our minds, we must use them to the full.[16] Intellectual sloth is as culpable as intellectual pride.

Christianity is certainly not a religion just for intellectuals, as some of the earliest heretics supposed. Christ came into the world to proclaim to *all* men the Gospel of salvation. Most of his original disciples and listeners were simple and unsophisticated people of limited education, as are most of those to whom the Gospel is proclaimed today. But however limited our abilities and education, it is our minds which must be fed, and our understanding to which the Gospel must be primarily, but not exclusively, addressed. This places upon Christian teachers a responsibility to provide a much more substantial content to their instruction than much that now passes for Christian education has to offer: and it requires of all who wish to consider and respond to the claims of Christ a readiness to apply their minds to wrestling with the great Christian truths as these have been received and transmitted from generation to generation. Although Christianity is for all, including the simplest of God's children, it is not, as many mistakenly suppose, a simple religion. At its heart there are the great mysteries revealed in the Incarnation, the virgin birth, Christ's Passion, death and descent into hell, his Resurrection and Ascension, and his abiding presence through the Holy Spirit in the Church. If there be a simple gospel, it is not the Gospel of Christ.

But for simple and sophisticated alike, understanding must always be complemented and completed by faith; and although faith means nothing less than total commitment, its intellectual element can never be excluded or ignored. There are some who will possess the ability to penetrate a little more deeply than others the meaning of the Gospel, but not even a genius can ever do more than scratch the surface of the profound truths which it declares. When our minds have grasped all they can, but *only* then, we can rest in a faith which far outstrips the puny capacity of any human intellect.

There are in every age men and women whose intellectual gifts and training give them an awareness, which others lack, of deep questions which they must ask, and to which they must strain to find honest answers. Such persons constitute only a tiny minority, but their influence in and upon the world is out of all proportion to their numbers. If the Gospel is to be proclaimed effectively to all mankind, the needs of these people cannot be ignored, and much will depend upon their conversion and witness to Christ. They will not be won, but will be repelled, by emotional appeals or by superficial ways of evangelism or worship which do violence to intellectual integrity. As one of them has written:

> The emotional approach to religion can be so *vulgar,* if uncurbed by intelligence and education.[17]

If there is a hint of intellectual snobbery in these words, there is none in the careful and considered judgement upon a campaign of an American evangelist expressed by Archbishop Garbett in his last address, just before his death, to the Bishops and other clergy of the Province of York:

> In a scientific and technical age, when a man begins to think seriously of religion, he will ask the question, 'Why?' To him the Christian faith must be explained and expressed in the language of the intellect. It is an imperfect faith which loves God with the heart, but not also with the mind . . . There are very few thoughtful men and women in these days who are not conscious of the intellectual difficulties in the way of a supernatural faith: and a faith which is based on emotion alone may be swept away easily by the storms of criticism . . . It is impossible to stress too strongly the need of evangelization in these days, but we must see to it that the evangelization is on the lines which appeal to the whole personality.[18]

5. *The Repudiation of Authority*

Authority is necessary because we are not only individuals but also social creatures. Community life is impossible unless authority is acknowledged, accepted and respected.[1] It is the power or right conferred upon some to enforce or influence the opinions and behaviour of others, and it implies a source from which this power or right derives. Those who believe in God claim that he is the only source from which all authority derives because he is the *author* or creator of all things. Any authority possessed by human beings is not their own; it can be exercised by them only as his agents, and justified only if used for his purposes and under his direction. Authority entrusted by God to men also owes much to the accumulated wisdom and experience of humanity, but it can be neither absolute nor immune from error.

> Authority was the sum of the experience of past generations, providing a starting point for future investigation and knowledge: but once that authority was regarded as infallible, it became a means of stereotyping error.[2]

Two kinds of authority are generally distinguished.

The first is disciplinary authority. This is exercised either directly or through delegates by civil, military or ecclesiastical systems of government. It is designed primarily, but not exclusively, to obtain the practical obedience of its subjects in their behaviour. Kings or presidents, and perhaps to a lesser degree bishops or moderators, are usually more concerned to secure conformity of conduct rather than belief from those whom they govern; they are unlikely to interfere with their thoughts unless these threaten to undermine their obedience.

The second type of authority is specifically designed to influence and control the opinions, beliefs and attitudes of those over whom it is exercised, or even to force them into a common mould. This is the authority which often promotes its purposes by brainwashing techniques, and is claimed by exponents of political and religious ideologies.

All human authority has its necessary limitations. Whenever it is clearly rooted in the wisdom and experience of the past, we are bound to respect it until and unless the presumption that it is justifiable is conclusively disproved. But even the conclusions reached by an overwhelming majority of our predecessors can be, and sometimes are, mistaken; and even when they are not, the instruments of authority appropriate to one period of history are not necessarily so in another. If God alone is the ultimate source of all authority, even the universal concensus of his limited and imperfect creatures cannot claim the infallibility which belongs only to him. No human system of thought or government, however venerable and respectable its pedigree, can claim perpetual, unqualified and uncritical acceptance of its authority. The time may come when it is plainly right for a long-established kingdom to be replaced by a republic.

In addition authority has its dangers. The risk of its abuse is obvious enough, and selfish men obsessed by the lust for power, position or possessions, and the determination to cling to them at any price, have made deep wounds upon the human race which may yet prove fatal. Less obvious than the risks run by those who hold authority are those incurred by people who too readily submit to it. The majority in any age place their essential humanity in jeopardy and stunt their growth as persons by tamely submitting their lives and thoughts to the authority of others in order to escape their responsibility for thinking and acting for themselves. Most of us shrink from paying the price of freedom, as Ivan Karamazov observed to Alyosha :

> Man is tormented by no greater anxiety than to find someone quickly to whom he can hand over that gift of freedom with which the ill-fated creature is born.[8]

Failure to acknowledge that all authority is from God, and that in human hands it is limited and dangerous, is a major cause of its repudiation. But the many contemporary challenges to leaders in national, ecclesiastical, commercial and academic life are due not only to their abuse of power but also to a shrewd suspicion of their incompetence. A persistent and widespread belief, particularly among the young, that the unsatisfactory world they have inherited is the result of the failure of those in power to use it effectively in the interests of all, is by no means without foundation. Dissatisfaction with those in authority, moreover, has led to the questioning of the very basis of authority itself. At a time when men and nations are acutely conscious of their right to freedom from many of the restrictions to which they have been and are still subjected, there is a popular idea – understandable but mistaken – that freedom and authority are mutually exclusive. If it is a matter of either freedom or authority, then it is authority that must go.

The erroneous assumption upon which this false antithesis rests is that liberty is identical with licence.

> Liberty has come to mean 'freedom to do what I like and to possess what I can pay for', and this is surely the road not to Heaven but to hell.[4]

Licence is totally selfish; its object is to profit the individual at the expense of the community. It implies that anyone can do what he likes without consideration for anyone else. In consequence licence can only breed conflict, for if each person simply pursues his own interests he will quickly come up against others who are doing exactly the same. Furthermore, licence destroys the very freedom which it purports to express and safeguard. A person who claims to be free to smoke, drink or take drugs whenever he likes soon loses any ability to abstain, and becomes the slave not the master of his addiction.

Liberty is very different. As all authority derives from God so real freedom can be found only in him. Human freedom, like human authority, can never be absolute. It is subject to limitations imposed by nature and society. Since we are human beings and not birds or fishes our nature does not allow us, without mechanical assistance, to fly in the air or to live under water. Because we are social creatures as well as individuals our personal freedom is limited by the equal right of other people to exercise theirs, and by economic and other circumstances inseparable from social life. We are not free to take a voyage round the world unless we can afford the fare, nor to marry the girl of our choice unless she is prepared to consent.

The limitations upon our freedom do not mean, however, that it is not real. A wide although not unlimited range of possible lines of thought and action is open to us in many situations. We are free to choose whether or not we shall become Christians or Buddhists, atheists or agnostics; to vote for any political party or none; to decide to take up some particular profession or sport; or to go to the theatre next Monday or Tuesday or both. One of the most effective ways of dealing with a determinist is to treat him as if he *were* one, and to deny that he has any choice in such matters!

> The freedom of persons, which is evident particularly in the biographical pinnacles of the mountains of history, remains a threat to every scientific account of historical events. It cannot be charted and remains a mystery to the observer of the drama of history, who must be content with statistical averages for the description of the main currents of history. Yet the endless variety and unpredictability of the historical drama are proofs of the reality of that freedom, supporting the introspective evidence of the actors themselves, who know that they make free and responsible decisions, though they are also conscious of all the determining factors which prompt and occasion decisions.[5]

Respect for authority is a condition not only of social life but of genuine freedom. Authority is an indispensable guide to the thought and behaviour of every individual, and it is folly to ignore its directions. Choices which are truly free must be informed. If we choose without knowledge we remain prisoners in the cage of our ignorance, like animals in a zoo.[6] We are not free to choose between Christianity and atheism, Conservatism or Communism, until we have done all that we can to learn what each really means. To choose any one without some knowledge of all is to make no real or responsible choice at all.

A man is not free if he cannot see where he is going, even if he has a gun to help him get there.[7]

A further distinction must be made between two different ways in which the claims of authority are enforced or asserted. Authority is *coercive* or *persuasive*. It is coercive when it attempts to compel the obedience of those over whom it is exercised without regard for their personal convictions or wishes. It brooks no opposition, and demands, 'Do this, or else.' It is open to question whether authority of this kind can ever be justified or reconciled with personal liberty. Its uncompromising claims which distort authority into authoritarianism are yet another contributory cause of the repudiation of all authority. People refuse to be told what they must believe (or pretend to believe), or how they must behave, unless they can be convinced that there are good grounds for the pattern of belief and behaviour which authority advocates. The 'permissive society' is a proper protest against the authoritarianism which makes too little effort to explain and commend the ideals and values which it is designed to preserve and promote. It is only natural that men and women refuse to accept that they should not indulge in drugs or promiscuity if these are presented to them without explanation as matters in respect of which their freedom is entirely overruled. They are more likely to give them consideration if they realize that indulgence in either may do extensive damage to themselves and others.

Persuasive authority may be powerful, but it is supported not by force or the threat of it, but by considerations calculated to secure our freely given agreement and support. This is *moral* authority which can be expected to win men's respect because it recognizes their personal liberty and ability to decide for themselves. It is designed to elicit that voluntary but disciplined obedience which it is the object of all genuine authority to promote. This is something which religious as well as civil authorities frequently forget to their cost; a fact which explains the revolt by many members of the more authoritarian Churches against their traditional dogmas and discipline. Such authoritarianism is not authority but a perversion of it, and the social consequences will be disastrous if the repudiation of the one leads to the rejection of the other. True authority responsibly exercised does not destroy but safeguards human liberty.

In the New Testament *authority* does less than justice to the significance of the original Greek word which it translates. *Exousia* explicitly denotes an authority which is derived, and points to God as its only ultimate source, whether or not this is realized by those who possess it. The word also includes the meaning *power, dunamis,* from which it is only rarely distinguished.[8]

Jesus answered [Pilate], 'You would have no power over me unless it had been given you from above.'[9]

Christ's whole earthly life is a sustained acknowledgement of the primacy of the authority of God the Father recognized by his consistent obedience to his will. Christ is both subject to and exercises that authority.

> For as the Father has life in himself, so he has granted the Son also to have life in himself, and has given him authority to execute judgement, because he is the Son of man.[10]

It is by the Father's authority that he preaches the Gospel, forgives sins, heals the sick and casts out devils; and this is the authority which he asserted when his actions were called in question by his critics, first in Galilee,[11] and later in Jerusalem.

> And they said to him, 'By what authority are you doing these things, or who gave you this authority to do them?' Jesus said to them, 'I will ask you a question; answer me, and I will tell you by what authority I do these things. Was the baptism of John from Heaven or from men? Answer me.' . . . So they answered Jesus, 'We do not know.' And Jesus said to them, 'Neither will I tell you by what authority I do these things.'[12]

This was not a clever evasion of a difficult question. Christ knew that no answer could mean anything to those who closed their minds to any possibility of admitting the claims of himself or his herald, the Baptist.

All who met Christ recognized the authority with which he spoke and acted; some attributed it to the devil,[13] others realized that it was divine.

And they were astonished at his teaching, for he taught them as one who had authority, and not as the scribes . . . And they were all amazed, so that they questioned among themselves, saying, 'What is this? A new teaching! With authority he commands even the unclean spirits, and they obey him.' . . . They were all amazed and glorified God, saying, 'We never saw anything like this!'[14]

Although Christ was uniquely endowed with the authority of the Father he respected the authority of others, however unworthy they might be of wielding it. He recognized that even the power of Pilate, who sat in judgement upon him, was held of God.[15] Pharisees and Herodians, united in an unholy alliance to try to trick him into a subversive statement, were given an answer which, although enigmatic, revealed a more responsible attitude than theirs to the *de facto* authority of Rome, and exposed the ambivalence of their own position.

But knowing their hypocrisy, he said to them, 'Why put me to the test? Bring me a coin, and let me look at it.' And they brought one. And he said to them, 'Whose likeness and inscription is this?' They said to him, 'Caesar's.' Jesus said to them, 'Render to Caesar the things that are Caesar's, and to God the things that are God's.' And they were amazed at him.[16]

It is significant, too, that he gave his highest approbation to a Roman official who possessed precisely the qualities of character and discipline required of all those who are entrusted with authority:

'Truly, I say to you, not even in Israel have I found such faith.'[17]

Nor would Christ himself evade ecclesiastical obligations which others had to accept; even when he would have been morally justified in doing so, he claimed no exemption.

. . . the collectors of the half-shekel tax went up to Peter and said, 'Does not your teacher pay the tax?' He said, 'Yes.' And when he came home, Jesus spoke to him first, saying, 'What do you think, Simon? From whom do kings of the earth take toll or tribute? From their sons or from others?' And when he said, 'From others,' Jesus said to him, 'Then the sons are free. However, not to give offence to them, go to the sea and cast a hook, and take the first fish that comes up, and when you open its mouth you will find a shekel; take that and give it to them for me and for yourself.'[18]

This is a significant incident which illustrates an important principle. Christ teaches us here that although we have our rights there are at least some occasions when we should not insist upon them. On other occasions he reminds us of another related principle : that we have duties, too, but cannot discharge our responsibilities by merely doing them and nothing more. We are to do much more than duty requires, and in more than a dutiful spirit.

'For I tell you, unless your righteousness exceeds that of the scribes and Pharisees, you will never enter the kingdom of Heaven . . . If any one strikes you on the right cheek, turn to him the other also; and if any one would sue you and take your coat, let him have your cloak as well; and if any one forces you to go one mile, go with him two miles. Give to him who begs from you, and do not refuse him who would borrow from you.'[19]

Even if the Sermon on the Mount is as simple as many suppose, obedience to its precepts certainly is not.

As the Father sends the Son into the world to reveal and exercise his authority, so the Son sends his disciples to share the responsibility of exercising that authority.

'As thou didst send me into the world, so I have sent them into the world.'[20]

Mission involves authority.

And he called the twelve together and gave them power and authority over all demons and to cure diseases, and he sent them out to preach the kingdom of God and to heal.[21]

'All authority in Heaven and on earth has been given to me. Go therefore . . . and lo, I am with you always, to the close of the age.'[22]

The Father's authority conferred upon the disciples by the Son is to be exercised in intimate and eternal association with Christ himself. It is a gift and trust to be used in obedience to the Father and to his glory, and not for their own glorification. This is not authority as the world understands and employs it. On the night before he died, Christ showed to his disciples the pattern of true authority by washing their feet.[23] But even this occasion did not eradicate from their minds the worldly notion of authority which impregnated them. Christ had to make its meaning explicit by word as well as action.

A dispute also arose among them, which of them was to be regarded as the greatest. And he said to them, 'The kings of the Gentiles exercise lordship over them; and those in authority over them are called benefactors. But not so with you; rather let the greatest among you become as the youngest; and the leader as one who serves . . . I am among you as one who serves.'[24]

The humility of Incarnation is not incompatible with authority, but is its foundation. Mission involves humble service as well as authority.

Christ's obedience to the Father's authority in no way restricted his liberty but gave it full scope. Throughout the Gospels, and conspicuously in the Passion narratives, Christ, as we have seen, is in command of every situation. He alone is truly free, and it is to set men free from their bondage to sin and death, as prophecy foreshadowed, that he came into the world.

'The Spirit of the Lord is upon me, because he has anointed me to preach good news to the poor. He has sent me to proclaim release to the captives and recovering of sight to the blind, to set at liberty those who are oppressed, to proclaim the acceptable year of the Lord.' . . . And he began to say to them, 'Today this scripture has been fulfilled in your hearing.'[25]

The liberty Christ possesses and imparts includes release for the victims of error who are as unfree as the sinful and the sick.

> Jesus then said to the Jews who had believed in him, 'If you continue in my word, you are truly my disciples, and you will know the truth, and the truth will make you free.' They answered him, 'We are descendants of Abraham, and have never been in bondage to any one. How is it that you say, "You will be made free"?' Jesus answered them, 'Truly, truly, I say to you, every one who commits sin is a slave to sin. The slave does not continue in the house for ever; the son continues for ever. So if the Son makes you free, you will be free indeed.'[26]

The liberty which Christ offers to men through his life, death and resurrection is a present possession which we can begin to enjoy now; but its full realization by us and all creation still lies in the future.[27] Yet it must not be confused with anarchy, which Paul was falsely accused of preaching.[28] It has nothing in common with the contempt for authority, discipline and order which passes for freedom today. We can find liberty only in submitting our lives to the authority of God, and only those who share Christ's obedience can find his freedom. For liberty is not the right to do as we like, but release from all that prevents our becoming what by the grace and providence of God we can be.

> The first freedom of choice conferred the ability not to sin; the new freedom will confer the inability to sin . . . it surely cannot be said that God himself has not freedom of choice, because he is unable to sin?[29]

Sinners who reject Christ's freedom and authority are slaves and perverts. Only the saints are proper people.

Human authorities can only win and command our respect and obedience if we can see some signs of its divine origin and nature in the kind of power they claim and in the way in which they exercise it. God's authority is inseparable from his love, by which it is consistently directed. When human authority is inspired by any other spirit it is degraded into authoritarianism, and cannot expect to gain recognition and support. This is no trite sentimentalism, for God who is love is also righteous, and the claims which his authority makes upon us – whether directly or through the agency of other men – demand discipline, self-denial and unspectacular perseverance. But we are not deceived by the hollow pretensions to concern for human welfare with which many in authority try to cloak their own self-interest and ambition. Authority founded on love can never attempt to secure our obedience by false pretences, or to compel it. Even at the level of purely personal relationships we cannot force others to love us or to share our tastes and enthusiasms. We can only seek to win their freely given response to our love. Genuine authority, as we see it in Christ, is always moral authority.

False ideas about authority and freedom, and their relation to one another, have combined with abuse of power to lead many to destroy freedom by repudiating all authority. Here again the Church has tended to go the way of the world in asserting over its members a secularized kind of authority which bears little resemblance to the pattern which we see in the life and teaching of its Lord. It is no accident that from the time of the first disciples disputes about authority have been responsible for many of the divisions in the Church, and still preserve them. No particular ecclesiastical tradition has a monopoly of the authoritarianism which seeks to dominate rather than to serve, and tries to impose rigid patterns of belief, behaviour and structure instead of winning acceptance by commending and explaining them.

> What God wants of his human creatures is not that they should be puppets, responding slavishly to the strings of ecclesiastical control, but that they should be free men, responding to his grace with a spontaneous movement of heart and will.[30]

Like Angelo, in *Measure for Measure,* we forget that we are only deputies holding another's authority in trust, and it goes to our heads.

> But man, proud man,
> Dress'd in a little brief authority,
> Most ignorant of what he's most assur'd,
> His glassy essence, like an angry ape,
> Plays such fantastic tricks before high heaven
>   As makes the angels weep.[31]

True authority is self-authenticating, as it is in Christ. The authority of the Church can carry conviction and win obedience and imitation only when it is – and is seen to be – that of him who came among us as a servant, in obedience to the Father, whose service is perfect freedom.

The authority of Jesus . . . is the root of the matter

. . . We accept Jesus' authority not because he holds any official position, nor even because he has been consecrated and appointed by God. His authority does not rest ultimately even on the resurrection, since . . . the resurrection confirms Jesus' divine authority only to those who have already responded to his message and his life. Jesus' authority rests on the unique fact of himself. The Church in turn fulfils her calling only as she lives by his spirit, which is God's own spirit . . . the Christian community has authority only by virtue of what it is.[32]

6. *Egalitarianism*

We hold these truths to be sacred and undeniable: that all men are created equal and independent, that from that equal creation they derive rights inherent and inalienable, among which are the preservation of life and liberty, and the pursuit of happiness.

The noble and familiar words of Thomas Jefferson, incorporated into the original draft of the American Declaration of Independence, have been endorsed by every champion of human liberty. Any who dare to suggest that the affirmation that all men are equal is subject to any qualification whatever run the risk of being branded as snobs and heretics.

It is certainly true that in many respects all men are created equal. By virtue of their common humanity each and all, irrespective of colour, creed or social status, are equally entitled to the same respect, rights and opportunities for developing and using their particular gifts and potentialities. But the suggestion that every individual possesses the same abilities and faculties is so obviously absurd that it should be unnecessary to deny it. Yet this is the basic false assumption upon which egalitarianism is based; that every person is endowed not only with equal rights but with equal gifts, and shares unqualified equality in *all* respects. Egalitarianism, which is a distortion of equality, contradicts not only human experience but the structure of creation. Nature in all its aspects consists not of innumerable undifferentiated elements but of distinct grades or orders of matter.

> The heavens themselves, the planets, and this centre,
> Observe degree, priority, and place,
> Insisture, course, proportion, season, form,
> Office, and custom, in all line of order.[1]

Since man is part of nature his present life must be lived in accordance with its laws, which impose upon human society the same broad pattern which can be discerned in the universe at large. He cannot with impunity ignore this pattern; but this is precisely what egalitarianism tries to do. Its pursuit is against nature, a wild-goose chase, which as history shows must invariably come to nothing. Egalitarianism has been the avowed object of most popular revolutions and of the ideologies which inspired them. Yet there is a certain inevitability as well as significance in the way in which the French Revolution produced Napoleon, and the Russian Revolution, Stalin. And contemporary Communism leads in practice to a total denial of the theoretical egalitarianism of Marxism. 'Why did we have a Revolution?' asks one of Solzhenitsyn's characters, the prisoner Doronin. 'To do away with inequality! What were the Russian people sick and tired of? Privilege! . . . Privilege spreads like the plague.'[2] He should not have been surprised. In any society at any time those who have extraordinary abilities in political or professional life, in science or technology, will gain positions, privileges and influence which others, equally naturally, will fail to achieve. It is a lesson from experience that we are slow to learn; egalitarianism is very flourishing today, and its assumptions are the basis of many of our political, social and educational programmes.

We see the influence of egalitarianism in many of our modern democratic institutions and procedures. The object of democracy is to secure the rights of every individual; but this does not mean that each one is equally competent to judge the method and the means by which that object is to be achieved. It is a democratic axiom that every man has the right to participate in electing those responsible for government. Yet the justice of the demand 'one man, one vote' is not as incontrovertible as the clamour with which it is asserted would suggest.[3] However hard it may be to devise a fair and practicable franchise qualification, it is not unreasonable to contend that there should be one. It is not self-evident that the right to vote should be given to an illiterate who is asked to judge on issues of which he is wholly ignorant; or that a profligate, who has shown himself totally incapable of managing his own affairs, should have a stake in those of the nation.

There is a growing and apparently irresistible demand today not only that all should have the vote (at an age which is being steadily lowered), but also that more and more people should participate directly in the ordering of civil, commercial and ecclesiastical affairs. We live in an era of more and bigger assemblies and committees, composed of more and more people who are less and less qualified to deal with the matters before them. The consequences are in the interests neither of the community nor of individuals. Responsibilities passed from committee to committee are usually discharged by none, and decisions go by default. Egalitarianism breeds bureaucracy, a clumsy and expensive form of tyranny which, because it discourages personal initiative and responsibility, is not even redeemed by efficiency. It is under the inexorable control of Parkinson's Law and the Peter Principle. Work expands so as to fill the time available for its completion. Every official rises to the level of his incompetence.[4]

Egalitarianism requires that when decisions can no longer be avoided they must be made by the majority, on the questionable assumption that *vox populi est vox dei*. This was one of the matters on which Kierkegaard felt strongly.

> He [Kierkegaard] had not been impressed . . . by democracy with its confidence in majorities. 'One hundred thousand millions, of whom every one is "just like the others", equals One . . . Only when there appears some one who is different from these millions, or this One – only then is it Two . . . Truth is always in the minority, and the minority is always stronger than the majority, because the minority as a rule is formed of those who really have an opinion, while the strength of the majority is illusory, formed by the gang who have no opinion.'[5]

It is significant, too, that some of the nations which have contributed most to the culture and civilization of mankind have been small. Israel and Athens are obvious examples.

In politics the influence of egalitarianism masquerading as democracy can be seen in socialism, and in education in the prevailing tendency to standardization. The advocates of a State monopoly and the abolition of public schools claim it to be inequitable that some children should have advantages denied to others even if they, or their parents, are prepared to pay for them. The principle of genuinely equal opportunities for all in education as in other matters is one with which few would wish to quarrel. But its practical application requires more careful consideration than monopolists appear to give to it. Their policy is based on the same false assumption that the potentialities and needs of all students are exactly the same; and this is clearly not the case. If every child receives an identical education, the brighter are sacrificed to the less bright and are condemned to the frustration of being denied an equal opportunity of developing their own particular and more outstanding abilities. Although it is arguable that the achievements of the less clever will be in some degree improved by their association with the cleverer, in practice the converse seems to be more probable. Clever children are more likely to be hampered by teaching methods adapted to the needs of those less clever, and their achievements will in consequence fall far short of what they might have been. This is a serious matter, for the quality of life in tomorrow's world – its culture, ideals and standards – will depend upon the contribution which today's children have been equipped to make to it. If the gifted few are given inadequate opportunities for developing their talents not only they but all mankind will suffer.

Egalitarianism in all its forms breeds the uninspired and uninspiring mediocrity which is a depressing characteristic of human life today. 'Your levellers wish to level *down,*' said Dr Johnson, '. . . but they cannot bear levelling *up.*'[6] It is then not surprising that although *charisma* is a word much in vogue, the contemporary world is conspicuously lacking in genuinely charismatic leaders. This rare spirit is often quenched before it can do more than flicker, by powerful circumstances which combine to discourage potentially outstanding individuals from becoming what they could be; instead they are forced into the common mould of debilitating mediocrity in which most men are always content to acquiesce. Egalitarianism encourages the delusion that we are nothing but members of the herd, sheep rather than men, and forgets that every person is unique. The few who, like Jonathan Livingston Seagull, have a clearer vision of their possibilities and destiny are ostracized by a society which is jealous of any of its members who refuse to settle for its own self-imposed limitations.[7]

It is jealousy (or envy) which is the underlying motive of those who confuse egalitarianism with equality, resent all privileges and abilities which they themselves lack, and reject a social structure which implies their own subordination.

> The disintegration of class has induced the expansion of envy, which provides ample fuel for the flame of 'equal opportunity'.[8]

Envy is essentially divisive because it has a peculiar capacity for sowing the seeds of suspicion and discord among men. It is doubly dangerous when, as so often, it is unrecognized. It is indeed one of the most destructive and deadly of the deadly sins.

> The dullard's envy of brilliant men is always assuaged by the suspicion that they will come to a bad end.[9]

It is not only murderous but suicidal. It destroys the envious as well as the envied.

The Church has not escaped infection by the pervasive climate of contemporary egalitarianism. Here again it has inherited its susceptibility from the past, and in particular from the Reformation. One of the original distinguishing marks of Protestantism is its repudiation of the hierarchical structure of society of which in the sixteenth century the unreformed Western Church was regarded as a corrupt bulwark. It is one of the paradoxes of Lutheranism and Calvinism that although they acknowledged the propriety – and indeed the divinity – of secular hierarchies (as did St Paul), they rejected this structure in the ecclesiastical order, although with no consistency or practical success. One of the main planks of the platform of reformed Christianity, with its emphasis on the importance of the individual, was the axiom 'every man his own priest', the claim that every person has direct and immediate access through the only mediator, Jesus Christ, to God the Father. This insistence is entirely understandable at the time of the Reformation, when many features of the life and organization of the medieval Church tended to obscure the unique mediatorial status of Christ by the inflated powers which it appeared to accord to his ministers. The initial rejection of the traditional orders of ministry was understandable; but the attempt to substitute parity of ministers was unsuccessful because it was against nature. All the reformed Churches soon became, and have continued to be, as hierarchical – or even more so – as the Catholic Church from which they separated, and produced their own hierarchies of ministers who usually differed from those whom they superseded only in their titles. Old priest became new presbyter; old bishop, new moderator.

In spite of this development, however, the Churches of the Reformation gave to their lay members much greater scope for participating actively in their worship, government and administration. This principle of lay participation has been consistently maintained and steadily extended in their practice. In consequence a distinctively Christian egalitarianism has developed with gathering momentum in these Churches alongside of that of the secular world. The visible effects of this tendency upon the Roman Catholic Church remained negligible until the inauguration of the Second Vatican Council in 1962. Since then they have been dramatic, rapid and cataclysmic, and all the Churches of Western Christendom have been transformed, for better or for worse, by the powerful infection of egalitarianism. In each and all of them the laity are urged, on theological grounds as well as for practical purposes, to take an increasingly active part in every department of Church life. Many functions traditionally reserved to ordained ministers are now exercised by lay men and women. Doctrinal and liturgical as well as many other matters are submitted to the judgement of synods largely composed of members whose competence to deal with them is limited. Different orders of ministry have in effect been largely replaced by a hierarchy of councils, and bureaucracy flourishes in the Church as in the world.

This process received added impetus in the Anglican Church from the Lambeth Conference in 1968. In a mood of euphoria and by an overwhelming majority it passed the following resolution:

> The Conference recommends that no major issue in the life of the Church should be decided without the full participation of the laity in discussion and in decision.[10]

Discussion is one matter and is always desirable: but

decision-making is another, and it is not clear that the two different things should necessarily on all occasions be combined. Hindsight suggests that perhaps this well-intentioned resolution and its implications were not sufficiently considered. Responsible decisions can be taken only by persons who are reasonably well informed about the matters at issue. It is one of the weaknesses of Anglicanism that many of its members are lamentably ignorant of the faith and practice of the part of the Church to which they belong, and of why they belong to it. This ignorance extends to a considerable number of its representatives at synods and councils. Observation suggests that some of them do not even glance in advance at their agendas, and fewer still appear to have given any preparatory study to important matters upon which they will have a share in deciding. It is hard to take seriously the proceedings and decisions of bodies so constituted, or to believe that they are likely to be receptive to the Holy Spirit or effective interpreters of his will for the Church. In the Church, as in secular society, popular assemblies can only hope to serve God and the community if their members do everything possible to recognize and equip themselves for their responsibilities.

The Bible begins by accepting and affirming the hierarchical structure of the whole created order. Creation is a pyramid, and man, by virtue of the unique nature and status given to him by the Creator, is set upon its apex.

> Then God said, 'Let us make man in our image, after our likeness; and let them have dominion over the fish of the sea, and over the birds of the air, and over

the cattle, and over all the earth.'[11]

The same pattern is reproduced in the (inseparable) civil and ecclesiastical life of Israel, the people of God. There is nothing egalitarian about a society which took for granted the status and authority of patriarchs, judges, kings, priests and prophets, as necessary parts of the divine dispensation. There is a further and important point here. The structure common to nature and society reflects a mysterious hierarchical pattern within the Godhead of the Creator, foreshadowed in the Old Testament and later disclosed in Christ, as three persons in one God. Although the three persons are co-eternal, the incarnate Son acknowledges his subordination to the Father who sent him into the world, and to whom he gives perfect obedience.

The Father is greater than I.[12]

By everything that Christ did and said, and by his loving concern for all whom he met, he made it clear that every individual is of equal and incalculable worth and dignity irrespective of his character. He is as consistent in his love for each sinner as in his abhorrence of sin, and it is for each as well as for all that he lived, died and rose from the dead. Yet Christ never did or said anything to suggest that all men were the same, equal in their abilities, or alike in the positions they were called to fill and the work they were equipped to do. Christ, as we have already seen, takes it for granted as self-evident that different people have different gifts and different responsibilities. He accepted and respected the status and rights of the civil and ecclesiastical authorities of his time. He chose only some of his followers to be his disciples, accorded them a unique position, delegated authority to them, and gave them special work to do; and by the numbers he selected he plainly endorsed the hierarchical structure of the Old Israel, of which the New Israel is the heir.

> And he appointed twelve, to be with him, and to be sent out to preach and have authority to cast out demons.
> After this the Lord appointed seventy others, and sent them on ahead of him.[13]

In Christ the people of God were reborn, and in the days of his earthly ministry the infant Church required little organization. The task of beginning to shape the pattern of its life after the Ascension fell, under his continuing inspiration through the Holy Spirit, to the Apostles. Their first action, the appointment of Matthias in Judas's place, had a double significance. It demonstrated that they realized that, in faithfulness to Christ, they must maintain a body of men who held a special position and responsibilities, and that by making up their own number to twelve they must emphasize the continuity of the New Israel with the Old.[14] Later they were to assign other and distinctive responsibilities to the seven in Jerusalem, and to elders whom they appointed over the local Churches which they founded.[15]

It is however in the letters of St Paul that the hierarchical structure of the early Church is most emphatically asserted and provided for. St Paul consistently maintains his own position as an Apostle, although he admits his unworthiness of it: and he roughly condemns those who questioned or disregarded his authority.

Am I not free? Am I not an apostle? Have I not seen Jesus our Lord? Are not you my workmanship in the Lord?
For I am the least of the apostles, unfit to be called an apostle, because I persecuted the church of God. But by the grace of God I am what I am.[16]

It is in his description of the Church as the Body of Christ that he fully expounds and articulates its nature and structure. The first Christian congregation at Corinth was only too ready to pick quarrels on any pretext. Before dealing with a series of different incidents which divided them, St Paul points out, early in his first letter to the Corinthians, that these were all due to jealousy which in spite of his previous admonitions clearly persisted.[17] Parties formed round different leaders who were jealous of one another.[18] One was jealous of his own father's wife, and seduced her.[19] But he devotes most of his attention to the insidious jealousy of one another's gifts which was widespread in the congregation and undermined its life and witness. In particular, exaggerated importance was attached to the spectacular and controversial gift of tongues, which clearly aroused the envy of all those who did not possess it.[20] This was the situation which St Paul makes the occasion of his long exposition of the nature of the Church.[21]

He begins by reminding the Corinthians that their attitude reveals not only jealousy but arrogance. They are behaving as if whatever abilities they possess are their own, whereas in fact they are *gifts* which they have done nothing to deserve.

Now there are varieties of gifts, but the same Spirit; and there are varieties of service, but the same Lord;

and there are varieties of working, but it is the same God who inspires them all in every one.

Then he turns their attention to something familiar to all, the constitution of the human body.

For the body does not consist of one member but of many.

As in the human body so also in Christ's Body, the Church, some members are more important than others; but the superficial characteristics of any one member are irrelevant. All are indispensable. Mutual jealousies among members of the Body of Christ are not only evil and divisive, but absurd. If any single member, however apparently insignificant, fails to fulfil his particular function, no one else is able to take his place; Christ's Body will be as maimed and impoverished as a man who has lost an arm or a leg.

If all were a single organ, where would the body be? The eye cannot say to the hand, 'I have no need of you,' nor again the head to the feet, 'I have no need of you.' On the contrary, the parts of the body which seem to be weaker are indispensable.

As jealousy is the denial of love and the root of conflict, so love alone can bind the diversity of Christ's members into the unity of his Body. It is not by accident but by design that St Paul's description of the Church is crowned and complemented by the great hymn in praise of love which immediately follows it.[22]

Neither in nature nor revelation can we find support for

egalitarianism. Both proclaim the hierarchical structure of the universe and society which many today are unwilling to accept. Perhaps this reluctance is at least partly due to the associations of the word *hierarchical* in the minds of many people. Some of these are certainly unfortunate; for it is unhappily true that many who have risen to the top in Church and State have not only achieved their positions by questionable methods, but have so abused their authority as to infringe the liberties of others. The word suggests the indefensible tyranny of absolute monarchs, feudal lords or prelatical bishops. But a principle which is essentially true cannot be destroyed by the abuse of those who in their own interests misapply or exploit it. The antagonism provoked by the word *hierarchical* cannot justify the rejection of the underlying principle which it defines. Its repudiation is an illogical refusal to face an immutable fact.

The Church follows not its Lord but the world if it slavishly embraces egalitarianism. Christians differ from many who do not share their faith by insistently affirming the equality of all men in many important respects, a truth which is basic for genuine democracy. But to go further by asserting that all men are the same in respect of their abilities is an illusion bred of envy and malice which in Christ we are pledged to renounce. We are not only social creatures, but also persons; and each one possesses his own intrinsic worth, dignity and potentiality to make his own unique and indispensable contribution to the life of humanity. We realize our own identity and freedom, as well as those of others, not by absorption into an egalitarian society, but by integration into a universe which is, in all its aspects, essentially hierarchical in its nature and structure.

7. *Conformism*

A conformist is a person who really has no life of his own. He imitates or acquiesces in the attitudes and behaviour of others, a chameleon who takes the colour of his environment and becomes an indistinguishable part of it. In some respects conformism resembles egalitarianism, with which it is often associated, but in others it differs. It rests upon the same false assumption that man is nothing but a social creature, and obscures the distinctiveness of each individual person who is swallowed up in the crowd; and it has the same effect of reducing him to a level of prevailing mediocrity by discouraging him from thinking or acting for himself.

> [In] crowds . . . individual differences between . . . members are temporarily suspended, their critical faculties anaesthetized; the whole mass is thus intellectually *reduced* to a primitive common denominator, a level of communication which all can share.[1]

On the other hand, whereas egalitarianism is an expression of jealousy, conformism – as we shall see – derives from different roots.

The herd instinct is one of the legacies we inherit from our animal ancestors, and has a powerful influence upon us all. We are like the guests at the Mad Hatter's tea-party who, although the table was large, all crowded together at one corner of it.

> We are the hollow men
> We are the stuffed men
> Leaning together.[2]

In spite of the highly sophisticated and (in some respects) advanced nature of modern civilization, the herd instinct is as strong today as ever it was, and is responsible for the tendency of most people to conform. They are frequently not aware of their conformity or the many factors which combine to produce it. Many militant nonconformists are conspicuously conformist in their nonconformity! We are very susceptible to conditioning by our companions and circumstances.

> Ordinary people . . . are the way they are simply because they are sensitive to and influenced by what is going on around them.[3]

Within the all-embracing community of mankind there is a natural tendency for birds of a feather to flock together; and we live in an age not only of large popular assemblies but of many small groups and societies of every sort and kind. Their declared purpose may be cultural, educational, religious, political, sporting or whatever, and they may be very successful in promoting it. But every group has in fact also another important and often unrecognized object: it is to satisfy the desire of people to find any pretext for getting together. Although groups and societies meet real human needs, and often serve the community as well as their members, they also have their dangers. A group may produce a genuine fellowship and *rapport* among those who belong to it at the price of cutting themselves off from those who do not. Members of a group may become so entirely preoccupied with their own shared interests and activities that they forget everyone and everything else; and they may develop a jargon and customs intelligible only to themselves. Groups can make their contribution to society only if they preserve their awareness of the larger community. A group which becomes too exclusive, too wrapped up in itself, is potentially divisive and destroys its capacity for contact with all who are outside it. The vision and range of interests of its members are confined to their own little world which may be but a fool's paradise. They lose touch with the great world of reality and add nothing to its life.

Popular catchwords in a gregarious age are *participation, involvement, identification;* and they have important things to say to us all. They remind us of our inescapable responsibilities to others, and of the danger of trying to contract out of them by selfish preoccupation with our own interests and affairs. Identification in particular denotes a capacity for putting ourselves in the position of other people, a sensitivity to them which is an indispensable condition of living and loving, of care and compassion, which is a distinctive quality of all truly human life. We cannot be any use to others unless we can to some degree through imagination and sympathy identify ourselves with them in their joys and sorrows, and understand something of what it is like to be in their circumstances. Yet our identification with them can never be complete, nor should it be. Our solidarity with others cannot destroy our own distinctive personalities. If we go too far in our efforts to identify ourselves with others we injure both ourselves and them. We undermine our own identity : and we lose precisely that degree of objectivity or detachment with which we must regard their situation if they are to receive the help they expect from us. Over-identification defeats its own ends.

The dangers of self-defeating identification are increased when we set too much store by doing things together and too little by doing them alone; when we fail to recognize our own need of privacy and others' right to it. This is certainly one of the characteristics of contemporary life. The (literally) undistinguished uniformity of the houses in which many people live, of the factories or offices in which they work, of the super-markets they patronize and the mass-produced goods on their shelves, of international airports and hotels, are only a few of the symbols of the gregarious lives which we are compelled to live and in general are content to accept. These are the circumstances which are breeding grounds of conformism. It is natural, if depressing, for people whose lives are so standardized to be satisfied with the limited ideals and objectives of their neighbours. They ask nothing more than to be able to keep up with the Joneses. If everyone else has a motor-car, a television set, a refrigerator, a swimming pool, we must have one too. If mini-skirts or long hair are in fashion then, whether we like it or not, we follow it. If all our friends wear jeans and do not wash, we must go along with them. If others spend Saturday afternoons at a football match and Sunday mornings in bed with the newspaper, any other possible programme is out of the question. Political labels mean little when all parties are equally committed to collectivism and differ only in the type which they offer. In literature and art plagiarism and pastiche have largely replaced genuinely creative work, and real talent is either rare or frustrated. In every department of life originality and distinctiveness are exceptional; imitation and conformism are the rule. The majority go the way of the world instead of contributing to shaping and changing it.

The attitude of the conformist appears to derive from a combination of fear and sloth. He is powerfully influenced by what other people say, and he is afraid of appearing to hold views or take actions which are likely to arouse criticism. He is concerned more with the image he projects than with the person he really is or could be, and is for ever looking over his shoulder to see what sort of impression he is creating. He may be quite unconscious of the extent to which he is dependent upon popular opinion; and his fear of others' disapproval reinforces his fear of being alone. His fear is often accompanied by the deadly sin of sloth, for the temptation to take the line of least resistance is always strong. It requires much more effort and determination, as well as courage, to take an independent line, than to go along with the crowd. Those who give way to the promptings of fear and laziness are unlikely to derive much from life, or to make any significant contribution to it.

The Church has not escaped the influence of conformism, which can be seen in many departments of its life. Concern for the healing of divisions between Christians, expressed in the search for visible unity according to Christ's will, has rightly been described as one of the great facts of the present century. Yet there is a danger that our proper concern for unity may lead us to seek to achieve it without delay and at any price, in ways which are not necessarily God's. And in this as in other matters we may in all sincerity seek his blessing on the plans we make, instead of giving our obedience to his will. It is easy but mistaken to assume that all Christians are already sufficiently alike in all essentials to warrant a single ecclesiastical structure to express a basic unity which we already share. This is exemplified by the popular clamour for reciprocal inter-communion which is becoming difficult to resist. Yet although this attitude is understandable and sincerely held by many, it could not produce more than a façade of unity which might for a time conceal, but could not remove, the deep divisions which still exist between us; and it is difficult to believe that this is the kind of superficial unity which is the will of God. Christ is the truth as well as the way and the life, and there can be no real unity for his Church which is not based on truth as well as charity. Substantial agreement about the meaning of such basic matters as the nature of Christ and the Church, the Bible, the Eucharist, ministry and authority, is surely a necessary foundation for enduring unity.[4]

Readiness to conform with the practices of other Christians without sharing their convictions is irrational and dishonest, and is likely to produce more divisions than it heals. Tolerance and indifference must not be confused. Tolerance is the disposition to be patient with and respect opinions and practices which differ from our own; indifference asserts that it does not much matter what anyone believes.

A tendency to regard truth as expendable and conviction as irrelevant has perhaps also contributed to the decline of different parties within the Christian Churches. There can be little justification for sectarianism which claims for any particular group of Christians a monopoly of truth as it is revealed in Christ and dismisses all others as totally mistaken. But it is only reasonable to suppose that different ecclesiastical parties have preserved elements of truth which others have neglected or obscured; and the claims of each must receive careful consideration if it is to make its proper contribution to the one Church of Christ, in which the fullness of his truth is proclaimed. We need not fear nor regret the disappearance of our labels – Catholic, Orthodox, Protestant, High Church and Low – provided that the complementary elements of truth which in the past they denoted are preserved in the interests of the whole Church.

Groups and societies are as common in the Church as in the world. The health and vigour of a Church or parish often seem to be judged as much by the number of its study, discussion and other groups as by the size of its worshipping congregation. There can be no doubt that the life of the Church has been enriched by societies which pursue and propagate their own special interests within it, and owes much to the few who by their zeal have emphasized the importance of worship, witness and evangelism, in which all its members should be actively involved. But a Church group, like any other, may become an exclusive *élite* whose members lose touch and sympathy with the rest of their fellow-Christians; their loyalty to the group may in effect replace that to Christ and the whole Church which it should promote and deepen. If in the past societies within the Church have contributed much to its life, it is possible that today their place and function should be at least reconsidered. If their number is multiplied and their usefulness uncritically taken for granted, they may impede rather than promote the unity and mission of the whole Body of Christ.

The recovery by the laity of their proper place in Church life is long overdue. Clericalization, which disregarded the privileges and responsibilities of the vast majority of its members, has increasingly distorted the nature of the Church at least since the Middle Ages.

The Reformation protest against it failed to produce any lasting improvement in this respect, since the Reformed Churches quickly became as clericalized as the Catholic Church. In consequence there are still many who identify not only ministry with the *ordained* ministry, but the Church with the clergy. When we hear somebody say that John Brown is 'entering the Church', he usually means not that John is preparing for baptism but for ordination. Much of the ineffectiveness of the Church is due to its failure to insist that every Christian by his baptism is committed to active participation in the ministry of Christ.

The reaction against clericalization is wholly justified, but there are signs today of its being carried too far. This can be seen not only in a growing demand that the laity should assume most if not all of the traditional functions of the clergy, but also in the obsessive desire of some clergy to be so completely identified with the laity as to obscure their own distinctive vocation. There are priests who appear to be almost ashamed of their identity and calling, by insisting on wearing lay clothes on any and every occasion. But their contention that the laity want their clergy to look, speak and behave in precisely the same way as themselves is at least open to question. It may well be that this breaks down some barriers, that it makes for easy relations and intercourse at any rate on a superficial level; but it is not clear that it necessarily achieves anything more. A bishop once remarked to a progressive young clergyman who was giving him the benefit of his views: 'If you dress like a layman what do you expect the laity to tell you – which your collar would have prevented their telling you – except dirty stories?' It is easy for the clergy to be unconsciously arrogant in assuming that they know what the laity want and expect of them. Perhaps some of them do want their priests to be and look exactly like themselves. But it seems equally reasonable to suggest that people in need of the kind of ministry they require of a priest expect him to be readily recognizable for what he is. There are at least some who find it easier to approach a priest with whom they are not on over-familiar terms, who is in some way different from themselves, and whose judgement and advice are likely to be reasonably objective. The truth of the matter is that genuine identification must go far beyond clothes, which may be nothing more than an empty substitute for it. The identification of such people as St Francis of Assisi and the Little Brothers and Sisters of Charles de Foucauld owes nothing to its accoutrements but speaks for itself.[5]

Christ identified himself with all men by becoming a man. The Son of God is also the Son of Man, a title which in the Gospels Christ frequently claimed for himself but was never applied to him by others. It is a title which in earlier literature had been given to the expected Messiah, but it is doubtful whether in our Lord's time it still retained this association. Christ may have used it, as it was perhaps used by Ezekiel, not only in a personal but also in a corporate and inclusive sense to describe the whole people of God. Although he was certainly aware of the Old Testament overtones, Christ's description of himself as Son of Man seems to show that he used it in order to emphasize the reality of his humanity :

> Since therefore the children share in flesh and blood, he himself likewise partook of the same nature

. . . Therefore he had to be made like his brethren in every respect . . . For because he himself has suffered and been tempted, he is able to help those who are tempted.[6]

There could be no other way to mankind's salvation than incarnation. But although Christ is true man, his identification with mankind could not conceal his uniqueness. All those who knew him, listened to his teaching and saw his signs, testified that he was not as other men are. All other men are sinners : Christ is distinguished by his sinlessness which, far from diminishing his sympathy with sinners, increased it. Although personally sinless Christ became so completely one with sinful humanity that he shared and carried the burden of our guilt without sharing our sins. Our sensitivity to sin is blunted because we are its slaves : Christ alone can see sin in its true colours precisely because he is completely free from it.

> For our sake he made him to be sin who knew no sin . . .
> For we have not a high priest who is unable to sympathize with our weaknesses, but one who in every respect has been tempted as we are, yet without sin.[7]

It is Christ's holiness, his perfect obedience to the will of the Father, against whom all others are rebels, which impresses men even more than his signs. Peter's reaction to the miraculous draught of fishes is significant :

> But when Simon Peter saw it, he fell down at Jesus' knees, saying, 'Depart from me, for I am a sinful man, O Lord.'[8]

Christ was no conformist, but neither was he an indiscriminate iconoclast. He came not to destroy but to fulfil the law.[9] But he refused obedience to arbitrary interpretations of its letter rather than its spirit, and the social and ecclesiastical practices to which this had led. He gave much of his time and attention to publicans and sinners. He worshipped regularly in the synagogues but rejected narrow sabbatarianism.

> And he said to them, 'The sabbath was made for man, not man for the sabbath; so the Son of Man is lord even of the sabbath.'[10]

Nor would he allow ritual practices to be substituted for moral integrity.

> There is nothing outside a man which by going into him can defile him; but the things which come out of a man are what defile him.[11]

He condemned his religious contemporaries who were more anxious to impress others than to serve God.

> They do all their deeds to be seen by men; for they make their phylacteries broad and their fringes long, and they love the place of honour at feasts and the best seats in the synagogues, and salutations in the market places.[12]

To the opinions of such men Christ was wholly indifferent although he knew that this would cost him his life, a prospect which filled his disciples with alarm.

> Then the disciples came and said to him, 'Do you

know that the Pharisees were offended when they heard this saying?' He answered, 'Every plant which my heavenly Father has not planted will be rooted up. Let them alone; they are blind guides.'[13]

By word and example Christ constantly reminded the disciples of the limits of identification and conformity. He warned them against imitating the ostentatious religious practices of the Pharisees, designed not to give glory to God but to attract the approval of other people.

> 'Beware of practising your piety before men in order to be seen by them . . . Thus, when you give alms, sound no trumpet before you, as the hypocrites do in the synagogues and in the streets, that they may be praised by men.'[14]

Yet their lives, like his, are clearly to exhibit that distinctive quality which men recognize as holiness.

> 'You are the salt of the earth; but if salt has lost its taste, how shall its saltness be restored? . . . You are the light of the world. A city set on a hill cannot be hid. Nor do men light a lamp and put it under a bushel, but on a stand, and it gives light to all in the house. Let your light so shine before men, that they may see your good works and give glory to your Father who is in heaven.'[15]

He told them another parable. 'The kingdom of heaven is like leaven which a woman took and hid in three measures of flour, till it was all leavened.'[16]

His prayer for his disciples is that they may understand

the meaning and cost of their vocation in and to the world, that they may withstand the pressure to conform to popular standards and expectations, and reflect something of his own unique holiness.

> 'I. have given them thy word; and the world has hated them because they are not of the world, even as I am not of the world. I do not pray that thou shouldst take them out of the world, but that thou shouldst keep them from the evil one. They are not of the world, even as I am not of the world. Sanctify them in the truth; thy word is truth.'[17]

Like our Hebrew ancestors we are called in Christ to be holy. This means that our attention must always be primarily directed towards God, the only source of holiness.

> And the Lord said to Moses, 'Say to all the congregation of the people of Israel, You shall be holy; for I the Lord your God am holy.'[18]

There are two elements in holiness. It signifies *wholeness*. God is complete, self-sufficient.

> He is whole; there is no blemish of disease in him, no poison of death.[19]

Our search for holiness in and from God is the pursuit of that complete wholeness of body and spirit which we see in his incarnate Son and can receive only from him. But holiness also denotes *distinctiveness*. God is unique, distinct but never remote from all that he has created. This element too is plainly revealed in his Son, who although truly a man, is not as other men are. Our commitment to holiness also demands that we should be different.

> 'You shall be holy to me; for I the Lord am holy, and have separated you from the peoples, that you should be mine.'[20]

Yet holiness defies precise definition. We see it supremely in Christ; and we catch glimpses of it not only in the biographies of great saints but also in the lives of a few men and women whom we meet. There is no substitute for it. Whatever other gifts we may possess, our lives will carry conviction and win others to Christ only if they reflect something of his holiness. The mistake of the Pharisees was to suppose that respectability is enough, and many of the failures of Churches and individual Christians are due to repeating it. At times and in places where church-going is still fashionable, many people are content to conform for the sake of appearances without realizing that anything more is required. When worship is generally neglected they abandon it for no better reason than that others have done so. Conformism and holiness cannot coexist. The one looks at others and at what they are thinking and doing; the other at God, what he is and means us to be. Respectability may produce reliable and responsible people, but it cannot breed saints.

In a collectivist age, when governments and their departments try to control more and more of our thinking and acting, the temptation to conform is powerful and the penalties for nonconformity are formidable. In totalitarian countries conformism appears to be not only an easy option but the only one. But the price we pay for it is the sacrifice of our humanity as persons and of any right to call ourselves Christians. Like Christ we are called to be in the world but not of it; to share its life but to make a distinctive contribution to it; to be leaven not lump, salt which retains its flavour. We are to be conformed not to the world but to Christ.

8. *Looking Forward*

By force of circumstances and not by design several weeks elapsed between the writing of the rest of this book and the concluding chapter. At the time this seemed to be both tiresome and unfortunate, for the dangers of repetitiveness and incoherence are increased by interruptions. In retrospect, however, this particular interruption seems, at least to the writer, to have had some value, although readers may perhaps not agree; for the circumstances responsible for it provided an opportunity for reflection upon what had already been written, as well as material for the conclusion to which it is intended to lead. I hope that the inclusion of a brief account of them will not be considered an entirely irrelevant digression, but that it will help to relate and illuminate some of the matters with which we have been concerned.

My wife and I had to make the long journey from Pretoria to Cape Town to attend meetings at which matters of considerable importance were to be discussed and decided. Our journey was really necessary, but how should we make it? We dismissed the idea of travelling by train which would be both slow and expensive. There was something to be said in favour of both the remaining alternatives. If we were to go by air we should get to Cape Town in three hours, but the enormous saving in time would cost the price of two tickets; if we travelled by car it would be much cheaper, but the journey would take us two days. We eventually decided to drive, but without much enthusiasm. It appeared to be a time-wasting and tedious prospect, particularly since speed restrictions imposed by the fuel crisis meant that over a distance of one thousand miles each way we must never exceed a speed of fifty miles per hour. We did not look forward to the journey or expect to enjoy it.

In the event – and against all expectation – we found the long drive both relaxing and rewarding. When we had done this same journey previously we had been intent on getting to the end of it. We had travelled faster than sight, and only now realized how much we had missed. Flowers by the roadside, which had been no more than a vague blur, were transformed into delicate patterns of blooms to which each contributed its own distinctive form and colour. For the first time we noticed the sharp outlines of far distant mountains, the ever-changing formations of clouds and the shadows they cast, smoke rising straight at dawn and dusk from African kraals, the spontaneous friendliness of children who ran to the road to wave to us as we passed, and the animals and birds that live in the waste lands which we had dismissed as uninhabited and devoid of all life. These things had always been there if we had but had eyes to see them. In addition there were other delights enhanced by their sheer unexpectedness. For hundreds of miles the road runs through the Karoo, where the traveller expects nothing but unrelieved monotony; for this is usually a parched and barren plateau where severe drought is the rule, all life seems extinct, dams are dry and streams are sandy ravines. Now after the best rains for years the desert had blossomed. Rivers were in spate, lonely farms were surrounded by green fields studded with pools of standing water, and poplars and willows in their autumn splendour shadowed overflowing dams which had given them new life. Yet although we were surprised by so many delights along the way, we never became so preoccupied with them that we forgot our destination, towards which steadily and unhurriedly we were moving : we spoke of the friends we should see, and the business in which we should be engaged. It was because we had enjoyed and been refreshed by the journey that we were better prepared and equipped than we should otherwise have been to meet the responsibilities which awaited us at its end.

This is, of course, a hackneyed and well-worn analogy. It has been used by men through the centuries since they first began to reflect and to express their thoughts, because they realized that to a unique degree it illuminates the mystery and meaning of life in terms of their own experience. They recognize that they are subject to changes, not only within themselves but in their environment, and constant change is a characteristic of any journey. The country through which we pass and the road we follow are never precisely the same from one moment to the next. Sometimes the way runs straight across an empty and featureless plain, then twists sharply upwards over a mountain pass : sometimes it is crowded, sometimes empty : now the surface is smooth, then rough and dangerous. But travellers change as well as the road. The conditions with which we have to contend, the direction we choose, the hazards we encounter, all combine to test our faculties and to develop our characters. The manner in which we respond, or fail to respond, to the challenges which confront us either makes or breaks us. Our growth and development depend on our determination to resist every temptation to give up, and to follow the road to our destination. Many of us will grow old before we reach the end of the road of life which is long, difficult and perplexing; for we come to junctions and crossroads at which there are many to give us conflicting advice about the direction we should take and the destination for which we should make. Some tell us that there are no reliable guides or maps, that each traveller is on his own with nothing useful that he can learn from the experience of other travellers. Others insist that we have no option but to go along with the crowd, without wasting time or thought on wondering where we and they may be going. Many will try to convince us that the journey is short, that the only sensible course is to enjoy it as much as we can while it lasts, because it and we end at death. Such suggestions are tempting because they appear to offer an easy way of attaining immediate and desirable ends; but the gratification they provide is never more than partial and temporary, and their promise is short-lived. Directions like this will not lead us far along the road, but take us down byroads which, however pleasant, turn out to be dead ends. There is no future in following any road except the one which will bring us to our destination.

We have already noticed that there are many people whose aim it is to live entirely in and for the present.[1] They refuse to face the fact that life is a journey and behave as if it is not. Others consciously or unconsciously adopt one or other of two attitudes to life. As a result of temperament, disposition, background, education or other factors, they can be distinguished as either *conservative* or *progressive,* and this distinction is observable amongst those who take part in politics, Church affairs, and many other departments of social life. It is indeed true that the same person may exhibit both tendencies in different spheres of his own life : we may (for example) be conservative in our religion and progressive in our politics, for few of us are conspicuous for our consistency.

This is no new thing. In every age there must have been some who looked back rather than forward, and others who looked forward rather than back. In times of rapid change like the present the contrast is more marked and the distance between them increases. The distinction between conservatives and progressives is, of course, very broad, and either label covers many shades of opinion. Nevertheless each possesses general characteristics in attitude and outlook which can be readily identified.

Conservatives are in varying degrees reluctant to acknowledge the necessary changes which life involves. Their great respect for the past is liable to distort their judgement and discrimination. They are inclined to idealize every tradition because it is traditional, and to criticize every innovation simply because it is new. Retrospect usually wears rose-coloured spectacles. Although they cannot escape change they are unwilling to accept it, and limp along the road of life with slow and flagging footsteps, impelled less by their own volition than by the irresistible pressures of the world and society. Understandably this is an attitude more characteristic of age than of youth, and it grows with our years. The older we get the slower in all respects we become; more attached to the past, less open to the future; less able to adapt to the novel and unaccustomed. But conservatism carried to excess is like disseminated sclerosis, which leads to total paralysis and death. It produces not persons but fossils.

Progressives are very well aware that life is a journey which involves constant changes, and they concentrate on the road ahead. They have a good deal of justification for turning their backs on a past which in many respects has bequeathed to them a thoroughly unsatisfactory legacy. The more extreme among them become radicals, intent on denying and destroying all the roots from which they have sprung, on the assumption that men can only set out on the right road by starting entirely afresh. But in their proper concern for the future they run the risk of travelling too fast, of travelling simply for travel's sake without enough regard for the direction in which they are going. The destinations they seek are often only vaguely conceived, and even when defined are not infrequently too limited. Many of them look for the end of the road in this life, in the setting up of an ideal society in this world. This is certainly a necessary part of God's design, but not his final purpose for mankind. The establishment of his kingdom on earth is a stage on our way but not journey's end. Those who settle for nothing more than an earthly Utopia are like travellers who abandon their journey by settling down to permanent residence in a roadside hotel. Many progressives look forward, but not far enough.

Both conservatives and progressives have become so entrenched in their respective positions, so convinced that there is no common ground between them, that mutual communication sometimes seems to be an impossibility. Their outlooks appear to be mutually exclusive and pose a straight *either* – *or* alternative. But this is yet another false antithesis. Each has something to teach and something to learn. Conservatives are right to insist that we ignore the lessons of the past at our peril.

Progressives properly maintain that we cannot be content to live in the past or the present, but must press forward into the future. Conflict between them has led to exaggeration and distortion of the positions which they are concerned to maintain, but this must not obscure the true insights which each possesses. Each must listen to what the other is trying to say; and we all have to listen to both if we are going to know more clearly where we are, and where we are going.

The Bible contains the accounts of many journeys. They are not only historical events but parables of life; and they share many common features. The call to embark on a journey comes invariably from God, and in the first instance to an individual. He is not usually required to travel alone but to take others with him. The travellers are well aware of the significance and purpose of their journey, and they take it seriously. They are prepared to meet difficulties along the way and determined to overcome them in order to reach their destination, however long the journey may be. They are on their guard against becoming so wrapped up in the problems and pleasures they experience on the road that they lose sight of where they are going. Faith and vision are their incentives to persevere to the end.

In the Old Testament Israel is engaged from the days of the patriarchs on journeys which had important consequences not only for those who made them but also for their successors. Abram is the pioneer pilgrim of the people of God.

Now the Lord said to Abram, 'Go from your country and your kindred and your father's house to the land that I will show you' . . . So Abram went, as the Lord had told him; and Lot went with him . . . And Abram took Sarai his wife, and Lot his brother's son . . . and the persons they had gotten in Haran; and they set forth to go to the land of Canaan.[2]

But Canaan was not the end of the road, and Abram's descendants were not permitted to settle down there permanently and undisturbed.

And God spoke to Israel in visions of the night, and said, 'Jacob, Jacob.' And he said, 'Here am I.' Then he said, 'I am God, the God of your father; do not be afraid to go down to Egypt' . . . Then Jacob set out from Beer-sheba; and the sons of Israel carried Jacob their father, their little ones, and their wives, in the wagons which Pharaoh had sent to carry him.[3]

God called the entire people to be travellers, and to travel together. Individuals who tried to evade their obligations to the community were recalled to their responsibilities. Moses fled from Egypt alone in search of peace and domesticity in Midian. In spite of his protests he was sent back by God to Egypt to rejoin his countrymen and to lead them out of bondage.[4] But Israel's deliverance from Pharaoh was followed by their slavery to self-will and disobedience; and in consequence of their faithlessness, inconstancy and pusillanimity their journey to the Promised Land was prolonged and arduous. When at last they reached Canaan it again proved not to be the end of their travels, and for the same reasons. Persistent disobedience to God and mutual strife eventually led Israel and Judah along their separate roads to exile in Assyria and Babylon.[5] These were catastrophes from which the Jews have never since completely recovered, for those who returned with Nehemiah and Ezra to their devastated homeland were no more than a remnant.

The Old Testament leaders in spite of their greatness were only human : they were unable to curb the disobedience of their people or to bring them finally to their destination and to the fulfilment of God's purpose for them. Israel was brought through experience of successive disasters to recognize that this was a task beyond merely human competence, and from the time of the Exile looked for one whom God would send to accomplish what even Abram and Moses had failed to achieve. Their expectation was fulfilled when God sent his Son into the world for the sake and salvation not only of Israel but of all mankind, that in him all men might know the way and be delivered from the disobedience which had prevented their reaching the Promised Land. God's own Son became truly man and has himself trodden the road which all must travel — from birth, through the world, to death and beyond.

> Thomas said to him, 'Lord, we do not know where you are going; how can we know the way?' Jesus said to him, 'I am the way, and the truth and the life'.

Christ calls all who would be his disciples to follow him in and through the world. We may not take the journey lightly, nor can we avoid the difficulties and dangers which he himself experienced and overcame. At the same time we have to remember that journey's end lies beyond the gate of death, which he opened, in Heaven, to which at his Ascension he returned.

> 'In my Father's house are many rooms; if it were not so, would I have told you that I go to prepare a place for you? And when I go to prepare a place for you, I will come again and will take you to myself, that where I am you may be also.'[7]

Christ's return to the Father did not mean – as perhaps the disciples feared – that he would abandon them to follow at a distance as best they could. He assured them that he would continue to be as close to them as he had been during his earthly ministry, but in a different way. His promise was fulfilled at Pentecost. Thenceforward and for ever Christ, who has triumphantly completed humanity's journey, is present through the Holy Spirit with the people of God as their constant guide and companion. No more for the New Israel than for the Old is the journey to be lonely or solitary. It is in the Church that Christ is most surely to be found. If we are to follow him we may not attempt, as Moses unsuccessfully did, to dissociate ourselves from the people of God, our fellow-travellers, however uncongenial we may sometimes find their company! But we have been given a clearer vision of the road and of our destination than the Old Israel ever possessed. The kingdom they sought in vain was an earthly kingdom, and their horizon was death. We have a leader such as they never had, who by his Resurrection and Ascension directs us beyond death to the Kingdom of Heaven.

> These all died in faith, not having received what was promised, but having seen it and greeted it from

afar, and having acknowledged that they were strangers and exiles on the earth. For people who speak thus make it clear that they are seeking a homeland. If they had been thinking of that land from which they had gone out, they would have had opportunity to return. But as it is, they desire a better country, that is, a heavenly one. Therefore God is not ashamed to be called their God, for he has prepared for them a city.[8]

What is man?

The answers offered are numerous, conflicting and confusing. But on one point there is general agreement. We human beings are, within the limits of our own knowledge and expression, unique in some respects which are obvious and beyond dispute. We know nothing like ourselves. We possess potentialities which if not unlimited are immense; their development has already produced phenomenal results in turning the resources of the natural world to serve our purposes, and the future possibilities open to us are beyond conjecture and imagination. Yet it is clear that our achievements have failed to bring us either social stability or personal satisfaction; for we are complex and many-sided creatures, and if any of our latent potentialities are denied scope and expression we are frustrated and unfulfilled. Our humanity is stunted and reduced if we are regarded (or regard ourselves) as nothing but creatures of our age, animals, individuals, members of the crowd, or cogs in a political or economic machine. Partial and temporary satisfactions can be no substitute for wholeness and integrity, and we cannot rest content with our present selves and circumstances. The penalty that nature exacts from all who refuse to go forward is atrophy and decay. 'He ceases to be good,' said St Bernard, 'who does not desire to be better'; and this is a truth which is not confined to the realm of morality. Yet experience shows us that change for the better is not an automatic process. We know that, although our liberty is not unlimited, we have some freedom to choose our course even when we are uncertain which one to take. It is this uncertainty which makes us too ready to accept easily accessible objectives which fail to fulfil their promise. Our achievements, although great, have failed to bring us to an understanding of what life is and what we are; and we have succeeded in creating a world in which we can discern many of the ominous signs which heralded the decline and fall of previous civilizations. Ultimately there are only two possible answers to the question, What is man? We are either pawns of fate or children of God. This is a true antithesis posing an authentic *either — or.* We have to make our choice and wager our lives on the truth of one or the other : and, as someone once said, we can neither decline the wager nor reduce the stake.[9] If we are nothing but pawns of fate our future is limited to a life which, in Hobbes' well-known words, is 'nasty, brutish, and short' : if we are children of God, our prospects are eternal.

Christianity proclaims that God is our Father, that on earth we are children indeed whose growth into maturity has only begun, travellers who still have far to go before they reach home. We can only find point and purpose in this life if we realize and remember the end for which God has created us. But the English word 'end' is ambiguous. In common usage it describes a terminus or conclusion, as when we speak of the end of a book or a journey. In this sense the word denotes destination. In another distinct but related sense 'end' signifies purpose fulfilled, as when we speak of a means to an end.[10] In this case the word means destiny. The phrase 'the end of man' includes both meanings, and when we use it the two analogies of life as journey and growth coalesce. Our destination is Heaven; our destiny is virtue.

'Virtue' is an unfashionable word and because it is often misunderstood is often used in a disparaging sense. A virtuous man is regarded as one who leads a sheltered life, immune from temptations, and deficient in real strength and virility. Virtue is identified with the escapism which Milton deplores:

> I cannot praise a fugitive and cloistered virtue, un-exercised and unbreathed, that never sallies out and sees her adversary, but slinks out of the race, where that immortal garland is to be run for, not without dust and heat.[11]

This is not virtue but a caricature. Indeed to speak of a virtuous man is really tautological, for the root meaning of virtue is manliness, the full flowering of all man's inherent attributes. A truly virtuous man is the only proper man, a Christlike man. It is significant that when Christ healed the woman with a haemorrhage it was recorded that virtue had gone out of him.[12] Men and women can only fully realize their humanity through contact with him in whom virtue is incarnate.

Our destination and our destiny are inseparable. We have been given life in order that we may follow the high road which leads us home to our Father and to mature manhood, resisting every temptation to turn aside down paths which lead to perversion, sub-humanity and self-destruction.

Unto wickedness men attain easily and in multitudes; smooth is the way and her dwelling is very near at hand. But the gods have ordained much sweat upon the path to virtue.'[13]

There is a striking similarity in the words used by the Christian and pre-Christian poets. Throughout the centuries pagan, Jewish and Christian writers have sought to express the meaning of life in terms of a road which every man must travel, undaunted by its dangers and determined to press on in spite of them; and they are unanimous in urging us never to become so preoccupied with the journey that we lose sight of our destination. Without the inspiration of a vision, constantly renewed, which evokes the response of all his faculties and resources no traveller can continue on his way. Here the message of the Bible is endorsed by the pagan philosopher who recorded his reflections on life's purpose long before most of its books were written :

When [the soul's] gaze is fixed upon an object irradiated by truth and reality, the soul gains understanding and knowledge and is manifestly in possession of intelligence. But when it looks towards that twilight world of things that come into existence and pass away, its sight is dim and it has only opinions and beliefs which shift to and fro, and now it seems like a thing that has no intelligence.[14]

The vision in terms of which – from the time of Christ – Christians have consistently conceived of man's destiny and destination is that of God himself.

Blessed are the pure in heart, for they shall see God.[15]

A century later these words are echoed by Irenaeus:

> The glory of God is a living man; and the life of
> man is the vision of God.[16]

So long as we are still travelling through this world the vision is never clear or consistent. The glimpses which we are given are rare and fleeting, and often unexpected. There are long stretches of the road which are dark and unilluminated, when the vision flickers and fades, and we are powerfully tempted to give up and go no further. It is through faith and hope, not through sight, that we find strength to persevere.

> I dimly guess what Time in mists confounds;
> Yet ever and anon a trumpet sounds
>   From the hid battlements of Eternity:
>   Those shaken mists a space unsettle, then
> Round the half-glimpsèd turrets slowly wash again.[17]

We cannot conjure up these moments of vision; but they come unsolicited and unmerited to every traveller who desires and determines to press on to the end of the road and often lifts his gaze to the horizon. It is by frequently pausing in stillness to rest in God and to set all our attention upon him that we become ever more receptive to the flashes of illumination sent to light up the road, and to keep bright the vision at its end. Those who abandon worship, or worship anything but him, destroy their capacity for seeing him.

We are children of God who has made us for himself, and in his image. We are travelling not to some unknown country but to our home, to the full vision of our heavenly Father, in whom we shall at last be fully and eternally ourselves. We cannot yet have any clear conception of Heaven, of what it will be like to have attained to mature manhood, 'to the measure of the stature of the fullness Christ',[18] which is our destiny. But our deepest aspirations and our glimpses of his glory assure us that only there and then shall we find fulfilment. Our Christian faith is eschatological, ever directing our attention to the end; it does not divert us from our present tasks, but inspires our resolution to see them through.

There are people now who profess the Christian name, and who are nevertheless ashamed of heavenly hope. The cry is raised, 'A this worldly religion.' There *may* be a bonus hereafter – only better not count on it. But I tell you that Christianity cannot for any length of time survive the amputation of such a limb as life to come. For God has put his infinity in our mind, and if we cannot stretch out for him beyond the little beginnings here allowed us, we must let go of God and loose him wholly.[19]

The difficulties of a journey are disheartening to a solitary traveller, and may seem insurmountable. The Christian is never alone, for he travels in company with the whole people of God. Although we make our journey through the world at different periods, temporal distinctions are transcended by the eternity of our destination. All the saints throughout the ages support us with their prayers, as we follow the same road which they too have travelled towards the vision which we but dimly see and they fully enjoy; for the pilgrim Church on earth is but a fragment of the family of God. Above all, we have in Christ a sure guide and ever-present companion. He leads us on to our destination, and is himself our destiny. For he is truly God who made us for himself; and he is truly man who is what each of us is destined to be, a true child of our Father in Heaven. This is the hope in which, with St Paul, 'forgetting what lies behind and straining forward to what lies ahead, [we] press on toward the goal for the prize of the upward call of God in Christ Jesus.'[20] We make for ourselves, and for all men, the ancient prayer in which the Church sums up the whole meaning and purpose of every human life.[21]

O Almighty God, who alone canst order the unruly wills and affections of sinful men : Grant unto thy people, that they may love the thing which thou commandest, and desire that which thou dost promise; that so, among the sundry and manifold changes of the world, our hearts may surely there be fixed, where true joys are to be found; through Jesus Christ our Lord.

Notes

1. INTRODUCTION

1. Heraclitus. Greek philosopher. Sixth century BC.
2. Cf. Teilhard de Chardin, *The Phenomenon of Man* (Collins, 1959).
3. *Tempora mutantur, et nos mutamur in illis.* Anon.
4. E. Gibbon, *Decline and Fall of the Roman Empire*, ch. 71.
5. T. S. Eliot, *Notes towards the Definition of Culture* (Faber, 1948), pp. 108, 19. cf V. Gollancz, *Our Threatened Values* (Gollancz, 1946).
6. Matthew 7:24-7.

2. THE CULT OF THE CONTEMPORARY

1. Acts 17:21.
2. Lord Acton.
3. J. S. Whale, *The Protestant Tradition* (Cambridge, 1959), p. 267.
4. Obvious examples are the reckless exploitation of the natural resources of the world, and popular indifference to the problem of pollution.
5. S. Neill, *Christian Faith and Other Faiths* (O.U.P., 1961), p. 178.
6. J. Pieper, *Hope and History* (Burns and Oates, 1969), p. 40.
7. The term the 'new theology' derives from a book bearing that title written by a Congregational

minister, R. J. Campbell, in 1907. It was revived after the publication of *Honest to God* in 1963, in which J. A. T. Robinson brought up and developed some of the ideas originally propounded by Campbell.

8. E. L. Mascall, *The Secularization of Christianity* (Darton, Longman and Todd, 1965), p. 1.
9. Hebrews 13:8.
10. John 8:58. cf. Exodus 3:14.
11. John 1.
12. Luke 4:21.
13. Mark 12:29-31. cf. Deuteronomy 6:4, and Leviticus 19:18.
14. Matthew 5:17.
15. Mark 2:27. cf. Luke 6:1-5.
16. Mark 1:21-6.
17. Mark 1:29-34.
18. Mark 5:24-34.
19. Mark 3:20-1.
20. John 18:10, 33-8. Luke 23:34.
21. Matthew 6:25-34. The mistranslation of the Greek *mē merimnate* in the Authorized version, corrected in the subsequent English translations, has been responsible for much misunderstanding. It is not forethought but anxiety which is here condemned as faithlessness.
22. Luke 12:16-21.
23. Luke 12:42-8.
24. Matthew 25:1-13.
25. Matthew 25:14-30, 46. Luke 16:19-31.
26. Matthew 24. Luke 12:49-56.
27. Colossians 3:18-24.
28. 2 Thessalonians 3:6-13.
29. The phrase 'the sacrament of the present moment'

was probably coined by J. P. de Caussade in his classic *Self-Abandonment to Divine Providence*. Rose Macaulay felicitously summarizes his teaching on this point: 'I like that idea, of each moment being an ambassador accosting us from God with a message how to deal with it.' She adds: 'Of *course* it enlarges life.' *Letters to a Friend 1950-1952* (Collins, 1961), p. 97.

3. SECULARISM

1. A. MacIntyre, *Secularization and Moral Change* (O.U.P., 1967), pp. 7-8.
2. A. Huxley, *The Perennial Philosophy* (Fontana, 1958), p. 208.
3. A. Huxley, *The Doors of Perception* (Chatto and Windus, 1959). His identification of his experience under mescalin with that of Christian mystics is critically examined by R. C. Zaehner in *Mysticism Sacred and Profane* (O.U.P., 1957).
4. One of the most influential of English linguistic philosophers is A. J. Ayer. See his *Language, Truth and Logic* (1936), and *Logical Positivism* (1959). cf. E. L. Mascall, *He Who Is* (Longmans Green, 1943), particularly p. 65, note 2; and J. V. L. Casserley, *The Christian in Philosophy* (Faber, 1949), pp. 186 et seq.
5. W. E. Henley, *Invictus*.
6. M. Wilson, *Religion and the Transformation of Society* (C.U.P., 1971), p. 13.
7. A. Solzhenitsyn, *Cancer Ward* (Penguin Books, 1971), p. 435.
8. W. Shakespeare, *Troilus and Cressida*, I, iii, 121-4.
9. M. J. Lapierre, 'Progress in Prayer' in *The Way,*

Vol. 10, No. 3, July 1970 (edited by James Walsh, S.J. and William Yeomans, S.J.), p. 234.

10. J. Maritain, *True Humanism* (Bles, 1938), p. 19 : Man, forgetting that in the order of being and of goodness it is God who has the first initiative and who gives life to our freedom, has sought to exalt his own proper movement as creature to the dignity of the first absolute movement and to attribute to his own created freedom the first initiative towards goodness.

11. A. Koestler, *The Act of Creation* (Hutchinson, 1964), pp. 388-9 : referring to and quoting from G. Kepes' *The New Landscape*.

12. A. MacIntyre, op. cit., pp. 68-9 : When theology is reinterpreted to make it relevant to the substantial secular life of the modern world, it always seems to lose any distinctive theological content and often too any logical consistency . . . The evacuation of the notion of God of its substantial content seems the only possible outcome of the whole Tillichian (or Robinsonian) enterprise.

13. 1 John 4:20-1.

14. Romans 8:20-1. cf. 2 Corinthians 5:17-19 : If any one is in Christ, he is a new creation; the old has passed away, behold, the new has come. All this is from God, who through Christ reconciled us to himself . . . that is, in Christ God was reconciling the world to himself.

15. 1 John 4:2-3; 2 John 7. cf. Colossians 2:20-3. The heresies which appear to be foreshadowed in these passages were later known as Docetism and Gnosticism.

16. Mark 6 :3. cf. Matthew 13 :55-7.

17. Mark 14:32-50.

18. Matthew 11 : 18-19. cf. Luke 7 :33-4.
19. Matthew 9:9-13.
20. John 2:1-11.
21. Matthew 15:32-8; Mark 8:1-9; Luke 9:11-17; John 6 :5-14.
22. Mark 2:1-12.
23. John 1:1.
24. John 5:43; 17; 20:17; Matthew 6:9; Luke 11:2.
25. John 12 :3-8.
26. John 18:36.
27. Matthew 6:10.
28. Luke 22:18. cf. 1 Corinthians 11:26 : For as often as you eat this bread and drink the cup, you proclaim the Lord's death until he comes.
29. John 6.

4. THE FLIGHT FROM REASON

1. W. Shakespeare, *Julius Caesar*, III, ii, 104-5.
2. Attendance at, for example, sessions of the General Assembly of the United Nations can be a discouraging experience. Many delegates appear to be concerned only to reiterate their entrenched positions. There is little real dialogue. cf. Napoleon : 'Three hostile newspapers are more to be feared than a thousand bayonets.' Quoted by M. McLuhan, *Understanding Media* (Sphere Books, 1967) p. 22.
3. 'Sensitivity Training in South Africa' – in U.S.P.G. magazine *Network*, February 1974, p. 5. cf. Another article in the same issue, p. 4, significantly entitled, 'The Most Helpful Experience of My Life'.
4. 'Betty said, "I'm lonely. I want to open myself to others but I feel I just can't take the risk." "Do you

really feel you want to take such risks?" I asked her. When she nodded I continued, "Are you prepared to take a risk now?" She nodded again and I left the group circle and went to one end of the room and I asked her to go to the other and then approach me and show me non-verbally what she felt about me. She gradually came towards me with the rest of the group looking on. When she reached me she put her arms round my shoulders and burst into tears of joy. She had taken a risk and found she was accepted.' (*Network,* loc. cit.) We do not know what happened to Betty after her course ended, nor what the consequences would have been if this became the pattern of her new behaviour.

5. 'From the fifteenth century onwards the *feelings* take an increasingly large place in the religious life. The intellect is not minimized, but illiterate peasants could not respond to rational explanations and logical expositions.' F. W. Dillistone, *The Christian Understanding of Atonement* (Nisbet, 1968), pp. 235-6.

6. John 11:5; Mark 10:21.

7. John 11:35-8; Luke 19:41.

8. Matthew 26:36-46; Mark 14:32-42.

9. Luke 2:49-50; John 5:30; Mark 10:32; Mark 14:36.

10. Mark 10:21-2.

11. Luke 11:27-8.

12. Matthew 26:33-4.

13. John 20:17.

14. Matthew 13.

15. C. S. Lewis, *Letters to Malcolm: Chiefly on Prayer* (Bles, 1964), p. 105. cf. Aquinas: 'In divine things our minds are bat's eyes before the naked light of the sun.'

16. 'It is the *duty* of the scientist to accept no pre-ordained limits but tirelessly to push his investigations as far as possible in every field of experience.' W. H. Thorpe, *Biology and the Nature of Man* (O.U.P., 1962), p. 6.
17. R. Macaulay, op. cit., pp. 163-4.
18. C. Smyth, *Cyril Forster Garbett* (Hodder and Stoughton, 1959), p. 403.

5. THE REPUDIATION OF AUTHORITY

1. 'The problems of authority and discipline are indeed involved in the art of conscious living, and are bound to arise wherever men dwell together in society.' K. E. Kirk, *The Vision of God* (Longmans, Green & Co., 1931), p. 3.
2. R. Jasper, *Arthur Cayley Headlam* (Faith Press, 1960), p. 106.
3. F. Dostoevsky, *The Brothers Karamazov* (Dent: Everyman's Library, 1957), Vol. I, p. 260. cf. E. Carpenter, *Common Sense about Christian Ethics* (Gollancz, 1961), p. 15: 'The cry for authoritative guidance is not usually healthy or adult.'
4. C. E. Raven, *Teilhard de Chardin: Scientist and Seer* (Collins, 1962), p. 191.
5. Reinhold Niebuhr, 'Freedom', an article in *A Handbook of Christian Theology* (Fontana Books, 1960), p. 144. Even an existentialist with no belief in God recognizes the reality, as well as the limits, of human freedom: 'Liberty is the very modal essence of existence . . . actual concrete possibilities vary from one person to the next. Some can attain to only a small part of those opportunities that are available

to mankind at large.' Simone de Beauvoir, *The Prime of Life* (Deutsch, Weidenfeld & Nicolson, 1963), p. 434.

6. Cf. A. Solzhenitsyn, op. cit., p. 541. Kostogltov observes that monkeys in captivity had lost not only their freedom but their capacity for it.

7. M. McLuhan, op. cit., p. 29.

8. Luke 9 :1. 'And he called the twelve together and gave them power and authority.'

9. John 19:11. cf. Romans 13:1 : 'For there is no authority except from God.'

10. John 5:26-7.

11. Mark 2 :8-11.

12. Mark 11 :27-33.

13. Mark 3:22.

14. Mark 1 :22, 27; 2:12.

15. See note 9 above.

16. Mark 12:15-17. Matthew 22:17-21.

17. Matthew 8:10. Luke 7:9.

18. Matthew 17:24-7.

19. Matthew 5:20, 39-42. cf. Anderson Scott, *New Testament Ethics* (C.U.P., 1930), ch. iii.

20. John 17:18.

21. Luke 9:1-2.

22. Matthew 28: 18-20. Even if Matthew does not give us Christ's exact words, there is no doubt that they express the substance of his final commission to the twelve.

23. John 13:1-11.

24. Luke 22:24-7.

25. Luke 4:18-21.

26. John 8:31-6.

27. Romans 8 :18-25.

28. Romans 3:8.

29. St Augustine, *De civitate Dei*, x, 30. Translated and quoted by H. Bettenson (Ed.) in *Documents of the Christian Church* (O.U.P., 1943), p. 81.

30. G. Caird, 'Relations with Roman Catholics : a Congregationalist View' in *Towards Christian Unity*. Edited by B. Leeming, S.J. (G. Chapman, 1968), p. 84.

31. W. Shakespeare, *Measure for Measure*, II, ii, 117-22.

32. J. A. Baker, *The Foolishness of God* (Darton, Longman and Todd, 1970), p. 353.

6. EGALITARIANISM

1. W. Shakespeare, *Troilus and Cressida*, I, iii, 85-8. cf. J. Huxley, *Essays of a Humanist:* 'Nature is not egalitarian.'

2. A. Solzhenitsyn, *The First Circle* (Fontana, 1970), p. 281.

3. There is substance in an aphorism of Dean Inge who defined one man one vote as belief in 'the plenary inspiration of the odd man'. Quoted by C. E. Raven, op. cit., p. 191.

4. C. N. Parkinson, *Parkinson's Law* (J. Murray, 1958); L. J. Peter and R. Hull, *The Peter Principle* (Souvenir Press, 1969).

5. A. R. Vidler, *The Church in an Age of Revolution* (Hodder and Stoughton, 1962), pp. 209-10. Cf. A remark of Sidney Smith in one of his letters : 'It would be an entertaining change in human affairs to determine everything by minorities. They are almost always right.' Arnold Toynbee frequently makes the same point in his *Study of History*.

6. J. Boswell, *Life of Johnson.* 21 July 1763.
7. R. Bach, *Jonathan Livingston Seagull* (Turnstone Press, 1972).
8. T. S. Eliot, op. cit. p. 104.
9. M. Beerbohm, *Zuleika Dobson,* ch. iv.
10. *The Lambeth Conference 1968 : Resolutions and Reports,* (S.P.C.K.). Resolution 24, p. 37.
11. Genesis 1:26.
12. John 14:28.
13. Mark 3:14-15; Luke 10:1. cf. Genesis 49:28 : the twelve tribes of Israel; Exodus 24:1 : the seventy elders of Israel.
14. Acts 1:25-6.
15. Acts 6:3; 14:23; 15:22.
16. 1 Corinthians 9:1; 15:9-10. Cf. The almost invariable opening words of his letters : 'Paul, a servant of Jesus Christ, called to be an apostle.'
17. 1 Corinthians 3:3; 2 Corinthians 12:20.
18. 1 Corinthians 3:4.
19. 1 Corinthians 5:1.
20. 1 Corinthians 14.
21. 1 Corinthians 12. cf. Romans 12:4-8.
22. 1 Corinthians 13.

7. CONFORMISM

1. A. Koestler, *The Ghost in the Machine* (Hutchinson, 1967), pp. 250-1.
2. T. S. Eliot, 'The Hollow Men,' I.
3. W. Sargant, *Battle for the Mind* (Heinemann, 1957), p. 181.
4. This has been accepted by the Anglican/Roman Catholic Joint Commission, which recognizes that

substantial agreement on Eucharist, ministry and authority are the necessary first steps on the road to organic unity between the two Communions.

5. e.g., Sister Renée, who made such a deep impression on Simone de Beauvoir. She was the daughter of a French diplomat who dedicated herself to the people of the *favelas*, the appalling slums of Rio de Janeiro, where she lived and worked until her death. S. de Beauvoir, *Force of Circumstances* (Deutsch, Weidenfeld & Nicolson, 1965), pp. 528-30.
6. Hebrews 2:14, 17-18.
7. 2 Corinthians 5:21; Hebrews 4:15.
8. Luke 5:8.
9. Matthew 5:17.
10. Mark 2:27-8. cf. Luke 6:5; 13:10-17; John 5:9-18.
11. Mark 7:15. cf. Matthew 15:18-20.
12. Matthew 23:5-7.
13. Matthew 15:12-14. This was a lesson which the disciples found it as hard to learn as we do. Peter sacrificed his loyalty to Christ to public opinion in the courtyard of the High Priest.
14. Matthew 6:1-2.
15. Matthew 5:13-16.
16. Matthew 13:33.
17. John 17:14-17.
18. Leviticus 19:1-2. cf. Leviticus 20:7; 1 Peter 1:16.
19. J. Goldbrunner, *Holiness is Wholeness* (Burns and Oates, 1955), p. 1.
20. Leviticus 20:26.

8. LOOKING FORWARD

1. Chapter 2 above, 'The Cult of the Contemporary'.

2. Genesis 12:1-5.

3. Genesis 46:2-5.

4. Exodus 5:15-23; 3:10.

5. 2 Kings 17:5-6; 24:10-16; 25:8-11.

6. John 14:5-6.

7. John 14:2-3.

8. Hebrews 11:13-16.

9. A remark made by Sir Walter Moberly in a talk on faith in Oxford many years ago.

10. This distinction corresponds to that between the Latin *finis* and the Greek *telos*.

11. Milton, *Areopagitica*.

12. Mark 5:30. cf. Luke 6:19; 8:46.

13. Hesoid, *Works and Days*, 287. Translated and quoted by F. M. Cornford, *The Republic of Plato* (O.U.P., 1941), p. 48.

14. F. M. Cornford, op. cit., pp. 214-5.

15. Matthew 5:8.

16. *Adv. haer.*, IV, 20, vii. Quoted by K. E. Kirk, op. cit., p. 1. This book is a penetrating study of the whole subject. He adds: 'Thenceforward, as we shall see, there was little question as to the fact. Christianity had come into the world with a double purpose, to offer men the vision of God, and to call them to the pursuit of that vision.'

17. Francis Thompson, *The Hound of Heaven*.

18. Ephesians 4:13.

19. A. M. Farrer, *A Celebration of Faith* (Hodder and Stoughton, 1970), pp. 164-5.

20. Philippians 3:13-14.

21. *Book of Common Prayer*, collect for Easter IV.